Parent's Guide to Youth Basketball and Beyond

Parent's Guide to Youth Basketball and Beyond

HOW TO NAVIGATE YOUR CHILD'S PATH TO COLLEGE BASKETBALL

Kevin Cantwell & Pat Alacqua

Parent's Guide to Youth Basketball and Beyond: How to Navigate Your Child's Path to College Basketball
Copyright © 2017 Youth Basketball and Beyond, LLC

First Printing, 2017
ISBN: 1536874671
ISBN : 9781536874679
Library of Congress Control Number: 2016912732
CreateSpace Independent Publishing Platform
North Charleston, South Carolina
Published by: Youth Basketball and Beyond, LLC
www.KevinCantwellBasketball.com

Copy and Text Editor: Jan Levin
Contributing Editor: Michael J. Pallerino

More Praise for This Book and Kevin Cantwell

"There are so many misconceptions about what kids of all ages should be doing to become better players and what coaches are looking for from players at every level to make their teams. Kevin Cantwell's years of player development and college recruiting experience make this book a must read for any basketball parent looking to learn what is best for their child."

– Jay Wright, Head Coach, Villanova University

"Kevin Cantwell, hands down, is one of the best evaluators of talent in the game. But it was more than picking out the superstars. Kevin could tell right away if a kid had what it took. He was good at finding the gems, the kids overlooked by other coaches. These were the kids that had real potential - the ones nobody was heavily recruiting - and Georgia Tech stayed competitive in the ACC because of Kevin's eye and the work ethic of these unheralded players."

– Bobby Cremins, College Basketball Coaching Legend

I have known Kevin Cantwell since my early days coaching college basketball in the ACC. His approach to the game, focusing on the development of a 'basketball I.Q.', is one of the first things we look for in a prospective student-athlete. Our program's success at the University of Notre Dame is built on having a knowledge of the game, understanding how to move without the ball and being a great teammate. The development that Kevin champions is key in creating the type of athletes that can succeed at the highest levels of basketball.

– Mike Brey, Head Basketball Coach, University of Notre Dame

"Kevin has years of experience in basketball skill development. He always has what is best for the athlete in mind. He knows how to best develop their skills. Kevin has always had a good feel on the landscape of college basketball and understands the nature of recruiting. He is a trustworthy person who knows how to showcase a player's talents. He has excelled for so many years because of his deep connection with basketball and a strong focus on how the game is taught and played."

– Tommy Amaker, Head Coach Harvard University Men's Basketball Team

"Kevin Cantwell is a friend, an excellent basketball coach, but more importantly a teacher. I have admired his work for many years. The Georgia Tech teams that Bobby and Kevin produced are some of the finest memories in ACC history. I would encourage all parents of aspiring basketball players to read this book."

– Mike Young, Head Men's Basketball Coach, Wofford College

"As a lifetime coach, Kevin knows that a player's skill level is what elevates that individual's effectiveness and basketball career. He is able to describe how perceptive coaches look at and evaluate prospects throughout the college basketball recruiting process. This involves evaluation of a player's skill set and basketball IQ. All parents would do well by closely following Kevin's insights on what is best for their child."

– Eddie Payne, Head Men's Basketball Coach, USC Upstate

"After covering major college basketball and the NBA for four decades, I've seen firsthand the deterioration of the fundamentals of the game of basketball as practiced by young boys and girls in high school. Finally, someone has decided to do something about it. Parents, I've known Kevin Cantwell a long time. His passion for the game and young people is second to none. Kevin knows what it takes. He knows what college coaches are looking for—at all levels. And he truly has the athlete's best interests at heart. He knows the college and high school game inside and out, and over the years has maintained and strengthened his connections to coaches and administrators. Kevin knows what he is talking about. I totally trust his character and judgement."

– Bob Rathbun, TV Voice of Atlanta Hawks and college basketball

"Kevin has written a wonderful and rare book that provides parents with the way they can alter their view of true learning for their children in the basketball arena. It brings the family into a true sense of supporting their child in a positive manner. He has given parents a real blueprint for what is best for their child. Kevin's level of knowledge is second to none. He has coached and worked with basketball players on all levels of competition. A must read for every basketball parent and a fan of the game."

"Kevin Cantwell is known in college basketball circles as an excellent recruiter who can evaluate and develop talent at the highest level. He has a "knack" for helping players improve their skill level and knowledge of the game. Any parent who has a child with college basketball potential will benefit from his understanding of the recruiting process."

"This book will have an amazing impact on youth basketball in the United States! Sports has such an important role in the development of our youth, having a "blue print" of the total development of a player is incredible! I have known Kevin Cantwell for 30+ years and his unbridled passion for teaching the game, the skill and sportsmanship is beyond compare. Having a guide to help players, coaches and most importantly parents understand the opportunity and requirements at each step of the way is unique.

As a longtime volunteer with the 128-year-old Amateur Athletic Union, I understand youth sports. We looked tirelessly for a "manual" we could incorporate in our AAU boys' and girls' programs. Every member of our planning committee was thrilled with the opportunity to use this book. This was and is exactly what we needed. The basketball purist in me recognizes we must continue to work on skill development. The AAU has made a very determined effort to create more skill academies, camps and clinics over the past two years. Incorporating all of Kevin's techniques and insights has helped us tremendously. Having personally witnessed Coach Cantwell's "on court" actual implementation of these skills and techniques at a recent AAU Nationals Championships, I saw how the parents learned as much as the players!"

My relationship began with Coach Cantwell when he recruited me to play basketball at Georgia Tech. Our friendship has grown through his support and loyalty during my playing career at Tech and the many years after. His honesty is something I could always depend on. He always communicates what needs to be said even when it might be something I or others may not want to hear. Kevin's dedication to the game and the relationships he has created around the game is hard to match. Any parent or player can benefit from his advice on what it takes to get better as a player and how best to manage the college basketball evaluation and recruiting process.

– Kenny Anderson, former Georgia Tech player and NBA All Star

"Kevin Cantwell is the best skill development coach I know. He has the ability to evaluate a player's skill set and customize a training program to assist in that player's basketball development. Kevin has an eye for talent and knows what it takes for a player to be successful at the next level. The interesting fact is that not all of the players he recruited to Georgia Tech were All-Americans out of high school. He had the uncanny ability to recognize recruits with "raw" talent and a "high ceiling" for growth as a player. His years of hands-on experience with the game is what makes him so good at what he does. BUT, what separates Kevin from every other coach is his ability to "connect" with people on the emotional level. Kevin understands the value of trust, loyalty and compassion in the player-coach relationship. As a former D-1 student-athlete who was coached by Kevin for 4 years, I can say Coach Cantwell is not just great at what he does, he is the best!"

– Jon Babul, former Georgia Tech Player, Director of Basketball Programs for the Atlanta Hawks

"Kevin was an assistant coach during my playing career at Georgia Tech. He was responsible for recruiting me out of California and signing me to play for Georgia Tech. I was a 175-pound skinny kid he believed could develop into a player that would compete on the highest level of college basketball in the ACC. During my redshirt year he worked with me to create a solid foundation of fundamentals to prepare me for my career at Georgia Tech. His focus with me was ball handling, shooting, balance, foot work, quicker release and even defense drills. I can honestly attribute most, if not all, of my success at Georgia Tech and my professional career to Kevin."

– Drew Barry, former Georgia Tech and NBA Player

"Kevin Cantwell has a gift for recognizing potential talent. Without his passion to develop my skills, I would have never gone on and played 15 years in the NBA. Kevin is the real deal. A great person and has absolutely no agenda other than to do what is best for others. His many years of college coaching along with his experience developing youth basketball players gives him a very unique level of knowledge and expertise. Kevin is an expert in guiding parents and kids through our youth basketball system."

– Jon Barry, former Georgia Tech and NBA Player, currently ESPN NBA Game/Studio Analyst

"This book is an invaluable resource for any developing basketball player and for their parents. For a player looking to get recruited to play college ball, being good is sometimes not enough. While I was not highly recruited in high school for college basketball, Kevin found me, saw something in me, and recruited me to Georgia Tech. Then he knew how to extract that talent. He sees things that no one else sees and understands things that other people don't understand. There is no one with more knowledge of how to develop a basketball player to the next level. Kevin knows exactly what high school, college and NBA coaches are expecting in their potential players, but more importantly, knows what it takes to excel in each of those levels. To my knowledge, there is not a book like this that gives such a roadmap for players and parents."

– Matt Harpring, former Georgia Tech and NBA player

"Kevin has a special ability to recognize and develop talent. His college recruiting knowledge and experience are great assets to players with the potential to play college basketball. Kevin's relationship network of college coaches is something any parent should tap into when trying to get the attention of college basketball coaches to recruit their child."

– Willie Reese, former Georgia Tech player/coach, current high school basketball coach

"Coach Kevin Cantwell has a wealth of knowledge about the game of basketball. He understands the process of college basketball recruiting and how to develop young players to reach their full potential. Coach Cantwell helped me develop from a junior college recruit to being a future NBA player. He is always filled with high energy and enthusiasm for teaching the game. I recommend all basketball parents read this book to help steer their kids to success!"

– Fred Vinson, former Georgia Tech and NBA player, currently assistant coach New Orleans Pelicans

"Kevin's many years of experience at the college level make him the perfect person to follow in terms of getting players evaluated and recruited. During my time with Coach Cantwell, I added different elements to my game that improved my ability to compete at the highest level in college basketball and later at the professional level. The subtle nuances of the game he has mastered is something dearly missed in today's game. Kevin is top of the line in terms of skill development and his ability to get players to buy into what he teaches. I've known him for 10 years and to this day I still use the drills I learned from him in every one of my workouts and workouts I conduct for younger players."

– Terrance Oglesby, former player at Clemson University, currently playing professionally in Europe.

"Kevin is always very easy to approach and talk with. His passion for the game is tremendous. He brings a great deal of knowledge and history to his training. I have watched him train not only my son, but many other kids. I truly believe he is one of the game's true masters of basketball training."

– Jeff Carpenter, parent of son playing college basketball

"Kevin has the knowledge on how to elevate a player's game to the next level. He is one of the main reasons I'm playing college basketball today. He gave me so much knowledge about the game and also taught me many things about life. I learned that if somebody wants to achieve their dreams, they have to work for it. The first time I trained with Kevin he told me I would never have the opportunity to play college basketball if I didn't put in the work to elevate my game. That statement stuck with me. It made me want to take my game to the next level. I now know I could have gone to a bigger school if I had just focused on my ball handling earlier in my childhood. Kevin showed me how to play the game and that there is more to it than just scoring. He taught me to pass better, dribble better and do all the little things that coaches look for."

– Spencer Norris, currently playing college basketball at Montreat College

"Kevin was always my sounding board. He was a mentor throughout my career, starting in seventh grade through my college years. He knows how coaches think. He has seen the good and the bad. I trusted his perspective on what was happening. It's not just the players who went on to play in the NBA, but the kids who played at all levels of college basketball that he helped drastically improve their game. My biggest improvement was in my footwork, balance and body coordination. Kevin taught me how to use both of my feet as equals in order to manipulate how my body could move on the court. Without his help, I would not have gone as far as I did. He genuinely cared about my development and helped me reach the goals I set for myself. He has a unique ability to connect with kids and parents. You don't see that too often today with coaches. He's in it for the right reasons."

– Ross Alacqua, former college player at Mercer University

"Both of our kids wanted to make their school teams, but had not played much. They had fun working with Kevin and looked forward to every training session. Even though there were several kids there, it felt like a one-on-one practice. They accomplished so much at every session. He even taught them how to work on their own in between training sessions. He has been a great resource for our kids. Regardless of how experienced your kids are, Kevin will have a positive influence on them. They will have fun and learn how to play the game."

– Scottie and Katrina Coggins, parents of a 5th grade son and 7th grade daughter

"Coach Cantwell was very helpful in my development as a basketball player. He took my game to another level, and I will be forever thankful for that. I love his passion for the game and his basketball stories. I wish I could have trained with him more when I was younger. He is a great teacher of the game."

– William Carpenter, currently playing college basketball at Milligan College

"Kevin was really helpful to my parents and me throughout the whole college recruiting process. He gave them insights into the college experience. He had so many stories and lessons he shared every time we got together. We had someone to lean on for guidance once coaches started showing interest in me. There isn't a single person I would recommend other than Kevin Cantwell. His knowledge of player development, mixed with his experience of the college level make his tutelage invaluable. He knew exactly how to make my game college ready."

– Chase Anderson, former college basketball player at Air Force Academy and Georgia College

"Prior to working with Kevin, I was not able to find a resource to teach the basketball skills my young sons needed. Kevin is very professional, easily approachable and very patient. The level of training was very good, because he emphasizes the basic skills that are not really taught anymore. Both of our boys loved working with him. They talk quite a bit about the exercises and how much they have learned."

– David Jones, parent of a 6th grade and 3rd grade son

"Kevin's one-on-one attention, his focus on weaknesses and his encouragement in the strengths of both my son and daughter were of great value. Their skills and techniques greatly improved; specifically, the shooting style my son learned. My daughter felt the program took her to a more focused level. Kevin has a genuine interest in the kids and their families. He was always responsive to anything we needed."

– Nancy Fox, parent of an 8th grade son and 5th grade daughter

"Kevin gave me a completely different outlook on the game – a perspective on how to evaluate my own game that I will never forget. Kevin taught me parts of the game that I would never have focused on. He guided me to focus on my basketball IQ and all the things I should do away from the ball. It was the little things that mattered. This helped me prepare for college coach evaluations. They were impressed with my footwork and how it advanced my game. There was so much more to the game than I had ever imagined. And Kevin made it fun. My only regret is that I wish I would have started learning with him sooner. It was the best decision in my basketball career. I believe any player who commits to learning what he teaches can accomplish any dream they have."

– Kaitlyn Wood, high school senior

"Having worked with Kevin, I now see my daughter doing things in games on a level most high school players can't do. Kevin immediately gave her the confidence to try new things. He has helped increase her speed of learning and showed her how to be a better teammate. He truly mentored her to not only be a more confident basketball player, but also a more confident person. Kevin has two gifts that give him the ability to work well with both kids and adults – a natural ability to read personalities and the gift of gab. When you hear your child say things like, "I love Kevin," and "I miss him," it sums it up. Two hours a week has made a lasting impression."

– Matt Ellsworth, parent of a high school junior daughter

"Before working with Kevin, my son would work out, but with no clear direction. We were looking for ways to elevate his game and believed he had the ability to play at the next level if he could get better in certain areas. Kevin clearly demonstrated and taught the things that helped my son reach his goal. He now plays at the collegiate level. Kevin's positive attitude helped reinforce my son's belief in himself. Kevin is a vast resource of knowledge and has the ability to help any young person reach his goals, whatever they may be. Anyone with a desire to reach full potential will never be disappointed when working with Kevin. His love for the game of basketball is second to none."

– Chuck Norris, parent of a son now playing college basketball

"I was not a super athlete. I had to rely heavily on my fundamentals, craftiness, and footwork to outsmart defenders. Coach Cantwell taught me new ways to counteract for my lack of athleticism. I learned taking time for me was far more pivotal than spending time playing 5 on 5 during the summer months. I wish I would have known more about Coach Cantwell's techniques at an earlier age. His involvement in my development was not only a blessing to me but to my family. He made it easy for my parents to trust his judgment. I think a majority of families struggle knowing about the pros and cons of the recruiting process and how we can be taken advantage of. Knowing what to expect while knowing warning signs can be critical for any family making imperative decisions for their child's future. My goal of playing Division I basketball could not have been done without the help of my parents, but my parents would agree it certainly could not have been accomplished without the help of Coach Cantwell."

– Madison Davis, played college basketball at UNC Ashville

"There are few people in the US basketball community with the knowledge, character, and personal experiences to impact players the way Coach Cantwell can. He has changed lives not just on the court, but off as well. The knowledge he is sharing in this book is simply a turnkey solution that every parent and coach must take advantage of. Kevin has the ability to explain the process as he has seen it first-hand. The value of this book is incredible!"

– Nathan Conley, former college player and NBA scout

"Coach Cantwell improved everything about my game. Especially with my footwork, shooting, dribbling and defense. I would not be the basketball player I am now if it wasn't for him. I am very thankful that I got to not only work with Coach Cantwell, but get to know him. I have improved so much. I have gained confidence while working with him. I have gained the confidence to go on the court and know what I am doing. I have learned so many new things. One of the best experiences I've had."

–Chyan Gallardo, high school senior

"I would never have been able to develop my game to the level I did without Kevin. Before working with him, I was a spot up shooter. I was having difficulty finding my shot while playing against more athletic players. After working with him, I became a completely different player. Through various leg coordination drills, I was able to train my body to move more efficiently, which allowed me to create more space for my jump shot. It also gave my legs the strength to stop on a dime and shoot while running full speed. He also taught me to pound my dribble harder and with more control. I know for a fact the Division I offers I received were a direct result of dribbling harder and training my legs and feet to move stronger. I was simply a more efficient mover on the court than most of my peers."

– Chase Anderson, former college basketball player at Air Force Academy and Georgia College

"Our two sons probably would have given up on the game if it were not for Kevin's great personality and making the boys feel comfortable. He really saw the potential in the boys and knowing someone saw it, they didn't give up! Not only does Kevin have knowledge and expertise, but also has a unique way of getting these kids to work harder and harder. When watching Kevin, you can tell how devoted he is to the children and the sport. Kevin is a true role model for kids of all ages. Very few coaches exhibit his character and expertise. We just can't say enough about this man. We all look up to Kevin!"

–Stephanie and Jeff Manka, parents of 7th grade and 9th grade boys

Table of Contents

More Praise for This Book and Kevin Cantwell ························· v

Foreword by Bobby Cremins ··· xix

Introduction ··· xxv

The Dream Can Become Reality for Your Child ····················· xxxi

A Basketball Life ·· xxxix

Section 1   **Grassroots Basketball – The Beginning of a New Era in America** ······ 1

Chapter 1   Nike Launches a Marketing Strategy ······························· 3

Chapter 2   A Spinoff Travel Team Idea is Launched ························· 7

Section 2   **Playing Basketball - How Good Can My Child Really Be?** ············· 15

Chapter 3   Treat Basketball as an Individual Sport ······················· 17

Chapter 4   Desire and Discipline = Quantity and Quality Learning ·············· 20

Chapter 5   Basketball IQ – Knowing Your Role – Scoring Points Overrated ······ 27

Chapter 6   What Kind of Player Should You Be? Emulate the
            International Player · 31

Section 3   Keys to Individual Skill Development · 37

Chapter 7   Parents Beware - An Obstacle to Individual Improvement · · · · · · · · · · · 39

Chapter 8   The Secret Ingredient for Individual Skill Development · · · · · · · · · · · · · · 43

Chapter 9   Shooting .... A Lost Art · 51

Chapter 10 Ball Handling · 55

Chapter 11 Defense · 62

Chapter 12 The Right Mindset - Building Your Game to UNLOCK
            Your Potential · 67

Section 4   Understand The Exposure and Evaluation Process · · · · · · · · · · · · · · 73

Chapter 13 Understanding the Odds of Playing College Basketball · · · · · · · · · · · · · · 75

Chapter 14 NCAA Takes Control of Travel Team Events · 81

Chapter 15 How College Coaches Recruit Players – The Process · · · · · · · · · · · · · · · · 86

Chapter 16 How College Coaches Recruit Players – The Decision Criteria · · · · · · · 103

Section 5   Parents - Your Role in Your Child's Success · 113

Chapter 17 "Team" Coach – You Need Realistic Expectations · · · · · · · · · · · · · · · · · · 115

Chapter 18 How Significant is the Coach? · 121

Chapter 19 Take Ownership. Know When to Lead and When to Let Go. · · · · · · · · · 126

Chapter 20 Beware of Negativity. Are You Part of the Problem or
the Solution? · 134

Chapter 21 Recipe for a Successful Life – Don't Miss Out by Being a
Spectator · 138

Chapter 22 The Competitive Journey for Your Child – Create The Plan · · · · · · · · · 147

Chapter 23 Knowledge is Power - Planning to Get the Attention of a
College Coach · 155

WHY - The Reason for Writing This Book · 165

It's Your Time to Get Started · 169

About the Authors · 173

Foreword by Bobby Cremins

College basketball recruiting gets so much media coverage these days that the average fan believes they know all the moving parts and ins and outs of their favorite programs. The truth is these daily recruiting tussles between coaching staffs of national powerhouses like Duke, Kansas, Kentucky, and North Carolina, among others, do not make the news, or the Twitter feed. This recruiting competition consumes the college coaching staff, 24 hours a day, seven days a week

I will never forget the meaningful wins, and the upsetting losses, throughout my coaching career. They are public knowledge, but the untold stories during recruiting are shared only among a few: the coaches and their families, the players and their families.

Kevin and I spent 20 years recruiting together at Appalachian State and Georgia Tech. We stressed over every prospect. We never stopped short of turning over every stone the NCAA rules allowed us to uncover. We were always seeking an opportunity to get to know a recruit. Staff meetings and traveling consumed most of the recruiting time. Influencing a prospect was all about visibility to confirm your sincerity through family visits and official visits by the prospect to our campus.

One untold story for Kevin and me was the recruitment of Kenny Anderson. Two years before we recruited Kenny, we signed Dennis Scott, the country's number one player. I must admit now; I was looking ahead. With Dennis on board, along with Brian Oliver, signing Kenny would give our Georgia Tech program a powerful backcourt.

Kenny became famous in the seventh grade. College recruiters, like Kevin and I (along with everybody else), started catching wind of the New York City Phenom. By the time he was a sophomore in high school, *Sports Illustrated* called Kenny the best player of his age in the country. When he finished at Archbishop Molloy High School in Queens, New York, the six-foot, two-inch guard was the first three-time Parade All-American since Lew Alcindor (Kareem Abdul-Jabbar). He ended his high school basketball career as the state's all-time leading scorer. To this day, there are many who will tell you they still consider Kenny the best ever to play in New York City.

We narrowed our point guard prospect choices to two players, Kenny Anderson and Bobby Hurley. Bobby was another high school All American who played for his father, Bobby Sr., at legendary St. Anthony High School in Jersey City, New Jersey.

In September, 1989, we had planned to make home visits to meet the families of two point guards on the same trip. We would see Bobby Hurley on Monday and Kenny on Wednesday. When we arrived in New York, we were told Bobby Hurley had visited Duke that weekend and committed to Mike Krzyzewski on Sunday. So all our efforts were now concentrated on Kenny. We were set to meet with him and his mother, but I was not very optimistic.

The race to get Kenny Anderson was a big deal. The three-year courtship to land this "once-in-a-lifetime" talent featured all the major Division I colleges, the superpowers of the game. Kenny narrowed his choices down to three schools, North Carolina, Syracuse and Georgia Tech – in that order, or so we thought.

The home visit we had with Kenny was shocking for us because he said Georgia Tech was his first choice, not Carolina. In an interesting twist, he told us the path to his recruitment should go through his mother and him – and nobody else. He liked us, and we could tell he liked us. But Kevin and I knew better. These are kids and kids change their minds.

Favorite or not, when we left the house, I turned to Kevin and told him, "Everybody needs to continue to think we are the third horse in this race, and you are going to be in Queens, (N.Y.) for a while." As long as Georgia Tech was considered third, the coaching staffs at North Carolina and Syracuse would not worry about us and counter our recruiting. They would focus on each other and not even consider us a real part of the conversation.

It was going to be a race to the finish line, which was signing day in November, and we were going to have a steady presence in New York.

Kevin was perfect for this assignment. A Queens guy himself, he was very familiar with the surroundings. His brother graduated from Molloy, and Kevin's high school, McClancy, played in the same league as Molloy.

So I knew if anybody could tend to Kenny, it was Kevin. I also understood sending Kevin full-bore into that recruiting storm meant he might have to be gone for a while.

But my gut told me it was worth the play. Even though it seemed he favored us, North Carolina and Syracuse couldn't be taken lightly.

Now, I'm not sure if the other schools camped out in a hotel room in Queens like Kevin did, but the excitement was real. When Kenny announced he was coming to Tech, we knew he was a great player, but we never imagined what he would do for Georgia Tech basketball. In Kenny's first year, we played in the Final Four (1990). With Kevin taking the lead, Kenny Anderson's commitment to Georgia Tech cemented our spot in college basketball's inner circle.

Kevin has a gift when it comes to recognizing talent and recruiting. He has few equals. Sure, it is easy to recognize the best players, but his insight into identifying kids with potential is second-to-none. There is a long list of players Kevin recruited, who he felt had capability and promise to play Division I basketball. Others would question his evaluation, but he was right more often than not, which is why Georgia Tech stayed among the elite in college basketball. His eye for talent goes back to our days together at Appalachian State.

It was Kevin's intuition and persistence that led to our coaching Matt Harpring, another one of the amazing players we had at Georgia Tech. He was unheralded, but Kevin saw something in Matt that kept our program thriving.

Georgia Tech was in Charlotte, N.C. preparing to play in the ACC tournament (1993), but Kevin stayed behind in Atlanta to watch the high school state playoffs, which were being held in Alexander Memorial Coliseum, our home floor at Georgia Tech.

Kevin wanted to evaluate juniors because our recruiting for the year was over. One of the teams Kevin watched was Marist High School, a local school that was undefeated. My son, Bobby, played for Marist. Kevin's plans were to leave for Charlotte after watching the first day of the state championships.

Harpring, a player on Marist's team, caught his attention. I personally saw Marist play a good deal while attending games to watch my son and thought Matt was a college prospect, but not on the ACC level. We also didn't have a need for a player at the forward position.

When Kevin arrived in Charlotte, he was relentless about why we should recruit Matt. He watched him outplay everyone in the tournament, leading Marist to a 33-0 record and a state championship. Kevin believed if Matt was willing to come to Georgia Tech knowing we had signed Mike Maddox, a high school senior from Atlanta who played the same position, what did we have to lose.

What happened next is mind-blowing. Matt Harpring's Georgia Tech career included these amazing accomplishments:

- Three-time First Team All-ACC
- First Team All-America (1998)
- Two-time Academic All-America
- Naismith Player of the Year (1998)
- Drafted fifteenth overall by the Orlando Magic
- Eleven-year NBA career

We had a great run, Kevin and me. He joined me as an assistant coach at Appalachian State in 1975, and later at Tech in 1986, and we rode side by side, all around the collegiate basketball landscape. In our 14 years together at Tech, we won the ACC title two times, appeared in twelve post-season tournaments, which included a trip to the Final Four in 1990.

I will tell you this, because I know it is true. Kevin Cantwell, hands down, is one of the best evaluators of talent in the game. But it was more than picking out the superstars. Kevin could tell right away if a kid had what it took to take on the rigors of the college game. He was good at finding the gems, the kids overlooked by other coaches. These were the kids that had real potential -- the ones nobody was heavily recruiting -- and Georgia Tech stayed competitive in the ACC because of Kevin's eye and the work ethic of these unheralded players.

Together, we coached in more than 800 college games, and recruited and taught 19 future NBA players. You recognize these names. Kenny Anderson. Stephon Marbury. Travis Best. Matt Harpring. Dennis Scott. The list goes on and on.

And it isn't just his knack for recognizing and recruiting talent that made Kevin such a great basketball mind. It is the way he worked so closely with every player and parent we recruited. He treated every single one of them the same way. He made them feel special. Kevin made them believe they were part of something that transcended the game of basketball. That means something, because when you ask these young men to stand by your side, it has to be for the long haul, through thick and thin.

Over the years, Kevin has remained one of my most trusted and dearest friends. When he told me about this book and the journey he is embarking on to continue to develop and guide young players, it made me reflect on all the work he has done in the game, and how much more there is left for him to do.

You would be wise to pay attention to every piece of advice Kevin Cantwell has to offer. The legacy he has created in the game of basketball can be found in the stories of every family he has helped walk through this process.

When you finish with this book, you will be light years ahead of those who did not open it up. Having the knowledge you will find in these pages matters to your future. Just ask the players and families Kevin has helped. It means everything.

Introduction

Throughout this book I will refer to the levels of basketball below college as "youth basketball," or, "grassroots basketball." My emphasis will be on what is important to accomplish a player's next basketball goal with the end result being the possibility of getting that college scholarship for your son or daughter, or making a team at another level along the way. I will give the structure for the right steps at the right time to ensure a positive experience.

I will provide a foundation of knowledge and the critical steps needed to successfully navigate your child's path to what is next. If your child is in the 4th grade, entering high school or a rising senior, it is important to understand how to accomplish his or her next basketball goal.

Think about it. What if you could discover just how good your son or daughter could be playing the game of basketball? What if you could find the step-by-step "how to" to make it happen? What if you could learn exactly what coaches are looking for from players they want on their teams? What if you could learn exactly what it takes for your child to make their middle school team? Travel team? High school team? What if you could find out how to get your child evaluated and recruited to play college basketball? What if you knew the role you needed to play to help your child succeed?

Despite the many theories going around throughout grassroots basketball in the US, the right answers to these questions have everything to do with the experience your son or daughter has playing throughout his or her journey at every level; middle school, Travel Team, high school and college.

There are accepted approaches recognized throughout youth basketball others see as the right path to answering these questions. Honestly, many are *not* the right path. I call these "myths for success." We will fully discuss these myths later on. I will share with you why many of these myths are not accurate. In the following chapters, I will guide you through the process of your child's journey. So often I see parents and players reacting to the many myths out there today, only to find out it is too late when they learn differently. Blame is being placed on coaches, teammates or other influences.

My goal is to prevent you from playing a role in the blame game by giving you the blueprint that will enable you to make the right assumptions and decisions, and take the right actions to navigate the right path for finding out just how good your child can be during their participation in the sport of basketball, ultimately helping them reach their dream of making the team at their next level and improve the odds of one day playing college basketball.

There is a process that can get you there. I've created and honed it over the last 35 years, and I'm going to share it with you in these pages.

The key takeaways you will receive after reading this book are:

- The step-by-step formula for your child to realize their potential.
- The clarity for the empowered role you must play so your child has the best chance for success.
- The knowledge for why the original intention for the grassroots system may not be what is best for your child.
- A comprehensive understanding of the myths you don't want to be following and how to sidestep all the "gotchas" before it is too late.
- Exactly what coaches look for from players at every level and how to use this knowledge to benefit your child.
- Understanding the evaluation and recruiting process from the college coach's point of view so you can give your child the best chance of getting the attention of college coaches.

The 3 Rights: Right Actions, Right Time, Right Resources.

Focusing on the right things at the right time and working with the right resources will give you the peace of mind you and your child need in the process.

Even if it is too early to be thinking too much about college basketball, it is never too early to be doing the right things along the way to lay the groundwork of competing and achieving at every level of your child's journey.

There is no theory in this book. Everything I am going to teach you is based on real world experience and results. My formula was created through trial and error, hard won experience of recruiting, developing and working with many players and parents who accomplished the same goals that are important to you and your child.

You are going to meet some of those parents and players in this book, because I am a big fan of teaching from, and by, example. You will note they are not hypothetical scenarios. I've read lots of books which use fictional case studies to explain methods, but this isn't one of them.

I will give you real world examples. I have to admit I enjoy bragging about the parents and players with whom I have worked. I love to talk about them and celebrate their successes. I believe competition and achievement through sports is a solid foundation for life success. It is why I am so passionate about what I do. It is all about helping parents help their kids use the sport of basketball to provide a path to a lifetime of success.

Obviously, that is not to say it is easy. There is plenty of hard work involved to accomplish a challenging goal. But my blueprint, my formula, has been proven over and over. It's the roadmap to a fast start and a successful finish. After all, if you're going to put in the work, it's nice to know you're using a proven process.

This book will not only enable your child to increase their odds of playing college basketball, it will also help you make the right decisions to enhance your child's experience while playing the sport, regardless of how far they go in reaching for the dream.

If your life is anything like mine, between work, family and all the other things in our lives, it often feels like there just aren't enough hours in the day. Because my time is so limited, I'm increasingly picky about the books I read. At the same time, I know it can often take just one idea for a book or resource to impact my life.

I believe Parent's Guide to Youth Basketball and Beyond: How to Navigate Your Child's Path to College Basketball is a resource truly worth the investment of your time.

When you apply what you are about to discover, the contents of this book will deliver what you need to know to ensure that you have no regrets after your child's basketball journey is over. There will be no regrets when it comes to what you could or should have done to positively enhance the journey and experience.

This book will give you everything you need to ensure you have a blueprint for your child's success. By the time you're finished with this book, you will have the formula to ensure your child has the best experience possible while striving to be the best he or she can be playing the game.

So without any further delay, let's get started!

Be sure to access bonus content as my gift to you

www.KevinCantwellBasketball.com/p/gifts

The Dream Can Become Reality for Your Child

"A dream doesn't become reality through magic; it takes sweat, determination and hard work."
- COLIN POWELL

The system for youth basketball in America is not a perfect one. I will tell you so much more about all this in upcoming chapters. The system was never intended to meet the needs of every kid who plays basketball. So many parents and players are just following the system – the way everyone else is doing things. At times, the system is not what is best.

Many kids playing basketball would be better served when parents learn if it is best to follow the system or to go outside it for a personalized solution. This book will enable you to know what is best to do in different situations, as well as what you should not do.

I want to share a story with you. The story is about a player who had a solid college basketball career. His basketball journey gave him a great foundation for life as a result of his reaching for the dream. This is a real life example of how a player and a parent made decisions. At times, they followed the system for getting things done. They also knew when to take the road less traveled to beat the odds for their basketball goals. This player reached his dream. He played college basketball by taking control and managing the system. He didn't let the youth system dictate his path.

If I had not already shared the end of this story, like most people, while it was playing out in real life, you would not believe the ending. You would think it was just not in the cards for this player to get a college scholarship and have a solid college career.

My role in this player's dream began in 1998. I started a basketball camp called "Invitational Basketball Academy" for fourth to eighth graders. At the time, I was coaching at Georgia Tech, but this camp had nothing to do with my recruiting role for Tech. Kids this young were not even on our radar.

My aspiration to have this type of camp came from conducting camps over twenty years at Appalachian State and Georgia Tech. I wanted a camp where all the participants had solid basketball experience. I wanted the opportunity to have an impact on these kinds of kids with my player development philosophies and methodologies.

Kids typically went to college basketball camps for a number of different reasons. Anyone could attend. For some kids, it was about being on a college campus. For others, it was because their parents were graduates. Basketball skill development often was just an afterthought. The individuals attending wanted to have a good basketball experience, but would leave frustrated and dissatisfied.

The kids who came for the basketball experience left frustrated, because they had to partner with campers for drills and games who were experiencing basketball for the first time. As college camp operators, our goal was to help everyone have a positive experience, but the player with experience gets slighted. The coach has to teach at the level of the kids who are unfamiliar with everything.

The philosophy of my Invitational Basketball Academy was to advance the teaching and coach the kids up so they had a productive and rewarding learning experience. The emphasis was on individual improvement. They participated in a curriculum that included college level drills and teaching methodologies.

My strategy for finding kids to invite to my Invitational Basketball Academy was simple. Get team rosters of players participating in winter basketball.

I arrived at one of my son's games early. This gave me a chance to watch the game before his. That was when this one player captivated me. I was not sure of his grade level. I assumed he was in the sixth or seventh grade, but this kid knew how to play. He was very unassuming, not fast or tall, but a very good ball handler. He had a nice shot with perfect form. He was an excellent passer and he had a great feel for the game.

After the game, I found out his name. He was the player I started telling you about at the beginning of this story. His name was Ross Alacqua. He was a seventh grader, and probably the best player in the league. I left the gym that night thinking Ross would be the type of player I wanted to attend my camp.

The response to attend the Invitational Basketball Academy was tremendous. My goal was to have seventy-five campers. I had to turn kids away, but Ross Alacqua ended up being one of the seventy-five. The camp lasted four days. The kids had a productive experience. Their parents were very complimentary and felt their kids had learned so much. Everything I envisioned and set out to accomplish was achieved.

Of all the parents I met, the one who intrigued me the most was Pat Alacqua, Ross's father. His teaching knowledge of the fundamentals was impressive, especially the importance of footwork, which is such a key piece of my personal philosophy for player development. Pat attended most of the camp sessions, and took notes on teaching techniques and drills.

I told him his son was very impressive and complimented him for what he had taught Ross – especially that shot. Ross's shot was so pure and fundamentally sound. You just didn't see that with many players at any level of play anymore, let alone from a seventh grader.

The following summer, Ross returned to my invitational camp. His skills had really improved. Pat and I also reconnected and picked up where we left off the previous summer. We discussed the importance of fundamentals. At the time, he told me he was going to purchase Georgia Tech basketball season tickets, so I knew we would see each other more.

My coaching career at Georgia Tech ended the following season. As I contemplated my next career steps, I pondered whether I would remain in college coaching or look at other possibilities in basketball. During this time, I stepped into player development training, which is where my deeper relationship with the Alacqua family started.

Ross was now in high school, five foot nine inches tall, and still an unassuming basketball player. He reminded me of other players I recruited throughout my college coaching career, and the times when others questioned my decisions. I often identified players who had real potential to keep getting better.

I envisioned Ross constantly improving because he had been taught the fundamentals from the beginning of his time playing basketball. He had such a strong foundation to build on, thus the potential for improvement was strong. Ross had the whole package: excellent fundamentals, an incredible work ethic and a real love for the game.

He was the ideal player to train, because he was committed to getting better. I always knew after our sessions together that he would work hard on his weaknesses until our next workout.

KEVIN CANTWELL & PAT ALACQUA

During Ross's high school basketball career, his talent was recognized by one of the best travel teams in Georgia, the Nike-sponsored Georgia Stars. While playing for the Stars, they primarily used Ross as a shooter. His playing time was sporadic, which frustrated him. I felt Ross's frustration, too, because I knew he was far more than just a shooter. Travel Ball is a fast flowing game, which is conducive to the more explosive, athletic players. This was not his makeup.

I knew Ross's entire game as good as anyone because of the personal training time we spent together, along with watching him play on his high school team. The "basketball powers to be" outside of our small circle saw him as a five-foot, nine-inch player who could "just shoot." I totally understood this perception, because playing with the Georgia Stars, that was his designated role. He did not have the opportunity to show any other offensive skills.

This personal frustration was turning into tremendous disappointment in Ross's mind, because of his love of the game and the time he had spent learning and working to build his skills and get better. Deep down, he knew he was a college player, but he felt he was never going to get any recognition.

Ross decided not to play for the Georgia Stars the summer before his senior year. This really upset his dad. I received a call from Pat telling me of the situation, along with his concern that the summer was the last time Ross could be seen by college coaches. The odds of him playing in college would get even worse, even doubtful if it would happen at all. Pat also was worried that Ross may have had enough of basketball and might quit the game.

I never believed Ross would quit, but his feeling about the Star's situation was totally understandable. I spoke with Ross. Our conversation was a short one. It lasted less than five minutes. I asked him why he did not want to play for the Stars. His response was simple. He said it was a waste of time to spend the summer months traveling, only to get frustrated. He still loved to play, but that was not how he was taught to play the game.

I totally agreed with his decision. Right or wrong, I had to respect his feelings. I did not question him. We discussed taking time off from our training sessions. Instead, we would focus on getting college coaches to evaluate his talent during the high school season.

I was such a believer in Ross that not only did I know he could play college ball, there was no doubt in my mind he could compete on the Division I level. So, for the first time since leaving Georgia Tech, I was back in my recruiting mode. It was just a little different now. This time, I was recruiting college coaches.

Our initial strategy was to look at Division I colleges that fit the level Ross could play, along with selecting the better Division II and Division III schools in the region.

College coaches typically don't randomly attend high school games, but I persuaded coaches I had relationships with to come and evaluate Ross. I was aware how coaches view a first time evaluation, especially one that is held during a player's senior year. If they are not completely sold on the evaluation, they most likely would not return.

Ross was the kind of player that did so many of the little things well because of his skills and basketball IQ. The more you watched him play, the more enamored you were with how good he was. The challenge was that if you could get a college coach to evaluate a player, their time was so limited you don't get the chance to make a second impression. You got one shot.

Knowing the type of player Ross was, I knew it was a long shot a college coach would be sold on recruiting him after one evaluation. Seeing all his skill sets in one game would just not happen. After one evaluation, coaches had some concerns. Is he a point guard? They were afraid of his size. They wondered if he could defend at the college level, especially against the size, strength, speed and quickness at the Division I level.

The coaches had legitimate questions and concerns. They could all be answered with more evaluations, but because of NCAA restriction for coaches on the number of days they can recruit, the second evaluation was not going to happen.

As Ross's senior high school season was coming to an end, some Division II schools were showing some interest, but there wasn't any positive response from Division I schools. It was becoming obvious to Ross and his dad the dream of playing on the Division I level was over.

My own recruiting experiences as a college coach told me the D-I dream still was alive for Ross. There are many recruiting stages coaches go through in one year. First, they are focused on going after their top recruit. Then, when they don't get that player, they reorganize and add candidates to their list. Failing again after focusing on the additional candidates, they now try and fill their open roster spots with a player they believe has potential, hoping that player will one day be good enough to play a meaningful role for them.

This type of recruiting scenario happens all of the time to coaches every year. This is why I was confident Ross still had a real shot at his D-I dream. At Georgia Tech, we found ourselves in this position often. We made some incredible decisions by taking a player who went beyond our wildest dreams on how good we thought he would be.

Entering the 1990-91 season for Georgia Tech, our number one choice for filling a roster spot was Brian Reese from New York City. During the early signing period in November, he committed to Dean Smith and North Carolina. We had to adjust our recruiting schedule in hopes of signing a player in April. The player we went after was Eddie Jones from Florida, who was not highly rated. In April, Eddie signed with Temple, where he had a good career, followed by a great career in the NBA.

Recruiting a good player for that position was not looking favorable for us. Our season lasted a lot longer than we anticipated, as we made it to the Final Four in Denver, eventually losing to UNLV in the semi-finals. During our time in Denver, Bobby Cremins was talking with NBA legend Rick Barry about his son, Jon, who had just finished his eligibility at a Texas junior college.

Immediately, we contacted Jon, knowing we had a few more days left to evaluate players. He informed us he was playing in an All Star game that week, which was our only chance to watch him. I arrived at the game early to watch warmups and get a feel for the type of player Jon was. It was going to be tough to get a good evaluation of Jon because the style of play in All Star games is offensively selfish with no defense.

From what little I saw I was impressed with Jon's skills in warmups. I was able to watch him shoot at half time. The only shot he took in the game was a fade away from the corner that was an air ball. I left without a solid evaluation opportunity.

Upon my return to consider Jon for a roster spot, our backs were against the wall. There was no more time to decide. Bobby asked me what I thought. I said let's take him. I made my decision on that one evaluation, with reservations and concerns on how good Jon was. His story ended up being a special one. Jon had two very good years at Tech and fifteen years in the NBA. Currently, he is an NBA commentator for ABC and ESPN.

Stories like Jon Barry were at the foundation of why Bobby and I were so successful during our time at Georgia Tech. It was all about having the confidence in the potential we saw in players – potential that could be realized at some point. This is why I was so confident in Ross's ability. I knew him better than any of the coaches evaluating him. There was no doubt he could play. We just had to get a coach to take a chance on his potential.

As I continued to help Ross, I reached out to my college coaching relationships. I continue to stay in contact with coaches to learn how the recruiting process is going. I get a feel for the progress in completing their rosters and always try to consider the possibilities of them not getting what they want.

I contacted Coach Mark Slonaker at Mercer University in Macon, Georgia. He had evaluated Ross, but had concerns. He asked if Ross would be interested in an offer to walk-on. Mark was very much in favor of giving him a roster spot with no scholarship.

Carson Neuman, a Division II school in Tennessee which was just coming off a D-II National Championship, had offered Ross a scholarship. He also had opportunities with Division III schools in Virginia. Ross decided to take the walk-on offer from Mercer, as he still believed he could play at the Division I level and wanted to keep reaching for that goal. He also wanted to prove to others who questioned his abilities that he was willing to take the risk. He believed he would earn that scholarship over time.

Not too long into Ross's freshman season at Mercer University, the coaching staff had plenty of time to evaluate his skill sets. They saw enough to believe he had potential to play a meaningful role for the team and decided to redshirt him the following year. The coaching staff was very impressed, so giving Ross an extra year was good for everyone.

Ross went on to have a very successful college career. He started earning significant playing time as he came off his redshirt year. He earned his scholarship. He had a key role in the playing time rotation during his junior and senior years, while also grabbing a spot in the starting lineup often throughout his last two years.

Ross reached for his dream and accomplished his basketball goals, but he received so much more. Let's not forget what I believe is the original intention for what sport participation is all about – the opportunity to learn life lessons, so you can use them to build a successful life.

Ross received what most kids have the opportunity to receive when they navigate their basketball journey with the right guidance around them. He received a foundation of life lessons that could be leveraged for a lifetime.

Upon reflection, Ross told me many lessons resonated with him throughout his journey. None was more important than persistence. Ross said,

"Persistence helped me face adversity throughout my college career and is still benefiting me in my business career today. Enjoy your accomplishments, but understand you need to get back to work. Life requires you to continue working and proving yourself over and over. Believe in yourself to keep going even when others are not currently recognizing you. It is all about persistence."

"It was clear to me I would always need to prove myself. When you don't get what you want or feel someone has not recognized your contribution, I learned I have two alternatives. Get upset and quit reaching for that something you want or work even harder to make the situation or person turn in your favor."

"Even as I started to play meaningful minutes during my college career and produce the results coaches were looking for, I had to keep proving myself every practice and every game. I was never going to be given the benefit of the doubt when being compared with guys that were six foot four inches tall and more athletic. All options would be exhausted before I was given a shot. I could never rest on my past accomplishments. My goal was to take any doubt away from the coach's decisions to play me more. I would force him to play me because of my hard work and results produced when he did play me."

The original intention of sports often is lost as everyone strives to win. It does not have to be one or the other. Our kids can get both. They can reach for the dream of competing and achieving and they can learn the right lessons for a lifetime of success. All they need are the right adults around them, with the right behaviors and perspectives.

I often tell parents and players when playing basketball, or any sport for that matter, the real value for the kids is not about getting what they strive for. The real value is about *not* getting what they want, and learning to cope with the adversity while continuing to reach for their goals when they aren't successful.

When playing basketball, more often than not, you do not get what you want. Just like life, it is all about your reactions to the ups and downs and your perseverance for what is important to you.

As you continue to journey with me throughout this book, I will share many insights with you. None will be more important than helping you extend your parenting role into the sports environment, doing everything you can to build a solid foundation of values in your kids, so that they live their entire life with those values while navigating the youth system so your child has the best chance at a positive experience and the satisfaction of reaching his or her potential.

No matter what my experiences are when dealing with young people, the joy of it all comes years later when they become successful as parents, or in their careers and other life accomplishments. It is just not all about the wins and losses. It is very gratifying to remember I was present along the way to see stages of their transformation unfold right before my eyes. Ross's story is one of those experiences for me.

A Basketball Life

"You have to take risks and be okay with failure.
Sometimes you'll win in style, and sometimes you'll lose big.
Accepting either result gives you a sense of calm."
– Jason Day, 2015 PGA Champion

was consumed with playing sports before I entered high school. I played basketball, baseball and ran track. My freshman year in high school I continued to play all three sports but I enjoyed basketball and for that reason, my skills continued to get better.

My enjoyment came because I could play basketball year round. All I needed was a ball and a basket. Baseball required at least one more person to practice. I got discouraged with track because my specialty was short distances. I would practice for hours during the week just to run for 20 seconds at a meet.

The era of basketball I grew up in was all about learning the proper way to shoot, dribble and pass. My teachers were the same people instructing today's young players: my father, friend's fathers and youth coaches. The difference was that everyone teaching the fundamentals back then knew the mechanics and techniques to teach the skills correctly. Kids couldn't make teams without a solid foundation in the fundamentals. No matter how young you were, constantly being taught those skills was a big emphasis. My continued improvement was the result of practicing dribbling and shooting by myself correctly.

My first attempt to make a team was in the 5th grade in a league called CYO (Catholic Youth Organization). I failed to make that team. Each grade level had an A and B level team. During my 6th grade through 8th grade years I played on the B level team and never made a starting lineup.

My High School Years

I started to get recognized for my talent while playing at Monsignor McClancy High School, located in the East Elmhurst neighborhood of Queens, New York. I continued to improve my skills during my high school years because I never stopped my desire to practice on my own.

McClancy was a private, all-boys Catholic school. The level of basketball was very competitive. The Catholic school league back then played the best basketball in New York City. My development progress was slow because of my body makeup. My height was okay at 6' 2" but my body strength had not kicked in yet. I played freshman, JV, and was in my junior season on the varsity when I got my physical spurt. That is when all of my individual skill development and practicing on my own met up with my body.

My junior and senior seasons were successful from a personal perspective as I made first team All Catholic School, but our team record was a disaster, finishing under 500 both years. Nonetheless, I was inducted into my high school Hall of Fame in 1997. It was a great honor.

My College Years

My dream to play college basketball became a reality when I received a scholarship to Gardner Webb Junior College in Boiling Springs, North Carolina. It seemed a million miles away from my stomping grounds in Queens. My love and ambition to excel started to take shape at Gardner Webb my sophomore year.

My freshman year was a big disappointment. It was a new experience for me as I spent more time on the bench than in the game. Our team was among the best in junior college. Artis Gilmore, tallest player in all of college basketball at the time, was on our team. He went on and had a fabulous NBA career, being named as one of the top 50 all-time NBA players.

My struggle through my first year was simply because my talent was not good enough for the level of college ball I was playing. But I never quit. I was determined to improve in all areas during the off-season. My goal was to get a scholarship to a four-year school.

It All Started by Accepting Larry Brown's Invitation

My entire life in basketball began to take shape the summer after my freshman year. At the time, I never imagined what was going to take place six years later.

I accepted an invitation from Larry Brown to work his camp the summer after my freshman year. He had just been named to his first coaching job at Davidson College, which, at that time, had one of the best basketball programs in the country.

Little did I know at the time, Larry would be enshrined in the Basketball Hall of Fame as a coach later in his career. He is also the only coach in basketball history to win both an NCAA Championship (Kansas in 1988) and an NBA title (the Pistons in 2004). Coach Brown played collegiately at the University of North Carolina and professionally in the ABA.

I happened to be working Gardner Webb's camp when I first met Coach Brown. He was a guest speaker at the camp. I was excited because my goal that summer was to do whatever it took to improve and gain knowledge on how to make that happen. Just the thought of working another college camp was exciting.

Upon my arrival at Coach Brown's camp and meeting other college players, I started to realize this was not your normal college camp. I was being introduced to some of the best players in college. This was very intimidating for me.

Pete Maravich's Influence

Here I was just 19 years old, a bench player from a small college. Many of the other counselors at the camp were some of the best players in the country. Charlie Scott and Larry Miller from North Carolina, Vann Wiliford and Nelson Isley from NC State, Dave Cowens, who was playing for Florida State, Brian Adrian and Mike Molloy from Davidson, Bob Verga from Duke, the team captain from South Carolina, Bobby Cremins, and the number one player in all of college basketball, Pete Maravich.

As I settled in I began to feel more comfortable with these guys even though the daily counselor games were extremely intimidating. My confidence on the court grew more and more each day but without a doubt the biggest highlight that enhanced my college playing career was watching Pete Maravich.

I was mesmerized with Maravich as he performed his dribbling and quickness drills for the campers. He explained the importance of each one of his drills, doing things with a basketball that I thought impossible. I took this new knowledge and incorporated it immediately into my summer lesson plan for getting better.

I didn't just learn the drills from Pete, but also the mindset of hard work. It still blows my mind what he could do with a ball and his hands. That alone taught me anything can be accomplished with hard work. Because of his influence, in my second season at Gardner Webb I started for the number one team in junior college.

My biggest accomplishment happened when I was rewarded with a scholarship to finish out my eligibility playing for the University of North Carolina-Asheville, an NAIA (National Association of Intercollegiate Athletics) college at the time in Western North Carolina.

A "Chance" Introduction to Bobby Cremins Changed My Life

During my time at Coach Brown's camp, the counselor I got closest to was Bobby Cremins. Bobby was one of the many New Yorkers Coach McGuire had on his team at South Carolina. Little did I know how this relationship would start a new chapter of my life at a future point in time.

Bobby and I had never met before, but he had heard my name from his teammates at South Carolina. Some of his teammates were friends who all attended Molloy High School who I played against. These included Kevin Joyce (future NBA and ABA player), Brian Winters (future NBA All Star and NBA coach), and Bobby Carver, a starter at South Carolina who went on to have a successful career in real estate.

Because Bobby and I were the same height, we found ourselves guarding each other a lot in the pickup games during camp. I remained on his radar after camp through my friendships with his teammates.

When my college playing eligibility was over, my coach at UNC-A gave me the opportunity to become a student assistant coach while I finished earning my degree. The opportunity helped send me in a new direction. I wanted to be a coach. I wanted to spend my life around the game I loved.

My thought was to be a high school coach, but I was told by high school administrators that I would be better served if I had a master's degree which was discouraging because I wasn't sure how to go about getting one. At the same time, I heard Bobby Cremins was going to take over Coach Mavarich's job (Pete's dad) as the new head coach at Appalachian State. At 27 years old, Bobby was the youngest coach in college basketball.

I wrote Bobby about becoming a graduate assistant coach, hoping he would remember me. He did. I received a call from him and, at age 26, my graduate assistant coaching journey started in 1975 at Appalachian State University (ASU).

My ultimate dream was to coach in college but I was working on getting my masters degree in order to become a high school coach. I received my degree in 1978 as well as getting hired as a full-time assistant coach at ASU. Bobby was having great success there, winning one Southern Conference Championship and one tournament championship, advancing to the NCAA Tournament.

My college coaching dream moved fast. In 1981, following six successful years at Appalachian State, Bobby Cremins was named the head coach at Georgia Tech. On the same day, at the age of 32, I was named the head coach at ASU. I became the youngest Division I head coach at the time. I was truly blessed. In just six years I went from wanting to become a high school coach to running my own college program.

But moving over one seat on the bench to being the head guy was not as easy as I thought. All the responsibilities now fell on my shoulders. I got an early lesson on humility!

My second game as a head coach was against Duke. Mike Krzyewski was in his second season as head coach for them. We won 75–70. That game was followed by a Jimmy Valvano coached North Carolina State team beating us 66-38. Welcome to college basketball!

In my fifth season after some tough years, it all started to come together. We finished with a 17-12 record. I was rewarded with a multi-year contract. I was also offered an assistant coach's position at Georgia Tech by Bobby Cremins.

As I thought through it all, it was a tough decision because I would be leaving a head coaching position for an assistant's job. When I decided to go with Bobby, many of my coaching peers questioned my decision because head coaching jobs are hard to come by. But I wanted the challenge to coach against the best, to recruit the best players in the country. It was also special for me to be back working with my friend, Bobby Cremins, the person I had started my coaching career with.

It seemed like a dream, especially for somebody who had never played Division I basketball. After spending eleven years at ASU, six as an assistant and five as a head coach, I was coaching now on the highest level in the most recognized conference in the country, the ACC.

I met the challenges in my new role at Georgia Tech and my decision to step down as a head coach was the best decision I could ever make. In my fourth season at Tech, Bobby promoted me to Associate Head Coach which was just another way he thanked me for all my hard work.

I had fourteen great years with Bobby at Georgia Tech. I had other opportunities for head coaching positions but none of the offers gave me the challenges I was

KEVIN CANTWELL & PAT ALACQUA

experiencing at Tech. I was going up against the best in the world every year and being touted by the media as one of the best, if not the best recruiter in college basketball.

My ego never needed the head coach's title. I was very grateful for what I had because we had a great ride. My college coaching career ended after twenty-eight years in 2000. I spent twenty of those seasons seated next to Bobby Cremins. It was special!

While at Georgia Tech we accomplished two ACC Championships, ten NCAA tournaments and one Final Four. From 1980-2000, we recruited some of the best players in the country – three times nabbing the nation's No. 1 high school player in America. Dennis Scott in 1987, Kenny Anderson in 1989 and Stephon Marbury in 1995.

During my time at Tech we had nineteen players reach the NBA: Kenny Anderson, Drew Barry, Jon Barry, Travis Best, Jason Collier, Eddie Elisma, Duane Ferrell, Matt Geiger, Dion Glover, Tom Hammonds, Matt Harpring, Alvin Jones, Malcolm Mackey, Stephon Marbury, Craig Neal, Ivano Newbill, Brian Oliver, Dennis Scott and Fred Vinson.

Over my twenty-eight years on the collegiate level, I saw a handful of major game rule changes. The three-point line. Extra bonus free throws. The shot clock. Each of these impacted my job.

In addition, the NCAA continued to change its recruiting rules which included when and how coaches could locate prospects to evaluate in high school, prep school, junior college and international. Little did I know how the recruiting rules changes at the time would have such a dramatic impact on our American youth basketball landscape.

A New Chapter in My Life

In 2002, I became the co-owner and Director of Basketball Programming at Suwanee Sports Academy, a facility with seven NBA-sized courts in Suwanee, Georgia, a suburb of Atlanta. During this time, Suwanee Sports Academy became a nationally known brand for being the place for players to train and compete in regional and national level tournaments.

My basketball journey took a turn during this new and exciting stage of my life. It gave me a first-hand look at the new viewpoints grassroots basketball in America had adopted. It took me a few years to fully understand exactly why the present generation of families were following new approaches both in high school and pre-high school.

My initial contact was with pre-high school families. I was amazed to find out the basic skills of footwork, ball-handling and shooting, once the cornerstone of every young player's foundation, were no longer considered critical factors in reaching a player's potential.

The new emphasis was on playing games. Parents and kids had grown to believe a quick tutorial on fundamentals, followed up with a lot of competition, is the remedy for constant individual improvement. They assumed the individual skills would evolve with age, believing that as their child got stronger, their skills would be easier to perform. The majority of pre-high school parents believe in this philosophy when it comes to teaching their kids how to shoot.

For the first time in my career, I was surrounded by a basketball culture I was not familiar with. All I ever knew was a mindset of "you train to play" to continuously improve and reach your potential. This new mentality believed "you play to train." This grassroots basketball world was also creating misconceptions about how college coaches locate players to evaluate.

As I shared my viewpoints with parents and players, my wisdom and experience fell on deaf ears. I couldn't accept this. I was watching a youth culture being directed by one myth after another. I was confident I could provide the right guidance for what was in the best interests of parents and players. This gave me the inspiration to leave college coaching to become an instructor which would give me a platform to educate parents and kids.

This was a new profession for me even though it still involved basketball. My biggest learning curve was realizing I had to be patient, trying to instill the mentality that individual training was a necessity. My first objective was developing a training program to teach kids on all levels the personal skills needed to improve so they could apply their new-found skills in game situations.

I believed I was making progress teaching parents their child's improvement would level off at some point without a solid foundation of basketball skills. But without fail, the majority would drop out to concentrate on travel ball.

I never got discouraged. I always had enough kids who chose the "road less traveled," putting training as the priority. I gave these players the tools they needed to work on their game, always guiding by telling them coaches at all levels make their decisions about players based on individual play. I encouraged them to put the time in to work on their own skills by themselves.

As players moved on in years through my training program, I added a college recruiting component. I was now back in my element but now recruiting colleges instead of players. I have successfully assisted many kids to live their college basketball dreams. My rallying cry became: "I will get a coach to evaluate you, but not until you are ready to be evaluated."

Kids and their parents are always trying to put the cart before the horse. A player should not be on the evaluation stage until they are ready. I know what college coaches are looking for. Having recruited players as a college coach myself, I understand in great detail what is and isn't important to them.

For the past 15 years, I heard parents and players of youth basketball talk about the path they are following to get the performance edge at all levels of play; elementary, middle, high school and eventually college. My experience, both as a college coach and player development instructor, has armed me with the tools to help players and parents understand what the right path is and what it takes to get to the desired endpoint.

Continuing My Journey

This book is the start of the next stage of my basketball journey. I am happy for those who are reading to come along for the ride. It is time to begin to look at changing the culture of youth basketball in America. This book is for those parents who want to leverage my years of knowledge and experience to help their kids accomplish their basketball goals.

I will use my knowledge, experience and relationship networks to continue this next stage of my basketball life in helping me to reach out to the masses. I want to connect with my readers and as many parents and players as possible.

I will share my formula for helping them reach the dream of playing college basketball. I also want to help you leverage the basketball success your son or daughter experiences with a college education which then can springboard them to a lifetime of success.

So many throughout grassroots basketball say the path to success is by playing games. Games. Games. Get some private lessons. Play on a Travel Team and get evaluated. There is a place for these things, but it's essential to know how to use them to maximize their benefit. And there is so much more to it.

This journey is for everyone, but mostly for those who love the game enough to work at what it takes to play at the next level which means the next level your son or daughter is at in school. It could be making the elementary team, middle, high school or college team.

I want to share everything I have learned about what it takes to be a better player and make teams. I want you as a parent to know exactly how to support your child's success in playing the game of basketball, leveraging the game to build a solid foundation of values and life lessons that can be counted on for life success.

So, if what I teach will be used to increase your child's odds of playing college basketball, I am confident it will be able to make a difference. If your son or daughter ends up not playing college basketball, but still uses what I can teach to enhance his or her basketball experience while playing the sport, I will be grateful for the opportunity to make a difference.

I look forward to helping parents navigate their child's basketball journey so they can leverage it for a lifetime of success.

SECTION 1

Grassroots Basketball – The Beginning of a New Era in America

> *"Your time is limited. Don't waste it living someone else's life.*
> *Don't be trapped by dogma – which is living with*
> *the results of other peoples' thinking.*
> *Don't let the noise of other's opinions*
> *drown out your own inner voice.*
> *And most important, have the courage to*
> *follow your heart and intuition."*
> — STEVE JOBS

The era of tournament basketball stormed into this country from all angles. It was exciting – the idea of playing for a championship trophy on weekends. Four to five games a weekend! Traveling long distances to play! Wearing the latest and greatest shoes and apparel. While young players were immediately attracted to this lifestyle with all of its positive attraction, the meaning of how to play the game got lost in the process.

These teams typically became members of one or a combination of non-profit youth sports organizations. The Amateur Athletic Union (AAU), Youth Basketball of America (YBOA) and United States Specialty Sports Association (USSSA) are just a few of these organizations in the US. They all have their own approach to tournament operations and how they go about sanctioning tournament operators.

AAU is often used in a generic way to describe all the teams and tournaments. This characterization is not an accurate way to discuss this segment of the youth sports industry. The focus of this book is not focused on AAU or any one of these organizations. The term "Travel Team basketball" or, "Travel Ball," will be used interchangeably to discuss this key segment of off-season basketball in the US.

The Travel Team concept was born during this new era of multiple games over the weekend. This popular model has had a big impact on grassroots basketball in the United States. These teams have met the needs and demand levels of a changing youth landscape wanting to play games rather than focus on learning how to play the "game."

Understanding why and how youth basketball changed will enable you to overcome the misconceptions that surround grassroots basketball.

In this section, I will explain how the Travel Team concept was the brainchild of Nike and Adidas to strategically market their shoes and apparel. Their Travel Team model focused only on the best high school players in the country. Their intent was for these players to be outfitted in the company's best products, then to compete against one another while college coaches from the best programs across the country evaluated their talent.

This section will also help you understand how the Travel Team concept transitioned into two different models, the one created by Nike and Adidas, and an expanded version born out of the increase of kids playing youth basketball in the US and their desire to become like the elite players. This expanded version created a grassroots movement that has changed the game in America. The youth system is not able to meet the objectives of all parents and players participating. I will tell you why so you can make better decisions for what is best for your child.

CHAPTER 1

Nike Launches a Marketing Strategy

"The difficulty lies not so much in developing
new ideas as in escaping from the old."
– JOHN MAYNARD KEYNES

n the mid-1980s, Nike introduced a strategy to market its basketball products to high school players. The goal was to influence young players early in their basketball journey. Giving them a place to play, shower them with basketball swag (footwear and apparel) and, hopefully, Nike could influence loyalty to the brand when they turned pro. Nike had hoped to replicate the success it found when it signed Michael Jordan right out of college.

The foundation of Nike's strategy was its basketball camp. The top 200 basketball players in the country were invited to participate in an all-expense paid camp that included complementary airfare and/or mileage and basketball gear. This first-of-its-kind basketball nirvana involved four days of competition between the best of the best in high school basketball. College coaches loved it.

The idea of watching the best play the best from around the country for four days was a college coach's dream. The competition enabled coaches to conduct good evaluations. Coaches from schools who could not recruit this caliber of player flocked to the camp to watch the games.

As the Nike camp grew in popularity, Adidas, one of Nike's biggest competitors in the athletic footwear and sports apparel market, started a similar camp using the same marketing strategy. A rivalry quickly ensued because both camps were held at the same time in July. Players had to choose one or the other. Soon, the race to see which player would attend which camp became a hot topic in the college coaching community.

Regardless of which camps the players chose to attend, coaches were now privy to more than 400 of the nation's best players through Nike in Indiana, and Adidas in New Jersey. College coaching staffs would split time between camps in order to evaluate as many players as possible in a short period of time.

From the beginning, the NCAA had been monitoring this new concept. The NCAA recognized high school players receiving free merchandise and other expenses from outside sources were in violation of its amateur rule. While the NCAA did not have jurisdiction over the companies, it did over the athletes who were subjected to losing their eligibility.

The camps continued for a few more years, but the players ended up having to pay their own travel expenses. They also were not allowed to keep the apparel they wore during camp. The new rules and regulations forced Adidas and Nike to rethink their strategies.

Still wanting to market their product without jeopardizing player amateur status, Adidas and Nike decided to sponsor their own teams. This strategy involved financing each team, which included providing the footwear and apparel the players wore. This was almost identical to the original concept with the difference being that sponsoring a team would not violate the amateur rule.

The game plan called for regional teams of seventeen-year-olds (17U) which included players of all ages with approximately twelve to sixteen players on the roster. The teams included the best players in that region. In addition, Adidas and Nike would sponsor tournaments in which only their teams competed against each other.

These tournaments immediately received a great deal of attention, which helped both companies build on their marketing strategies. This format was the beginning of real change for the sport. More and more tournaments were launched, and more and more teams were created.

The number of regional teams grew quickly. Larger populated areas fielded more teams. Soon, the sponsors started sixteen-year-old teams (16U), even though the best sixteen year olds were found on the 17U rosters.

And, other apparel companies also followed Nike's and Adidas' example. The additional teams allowed more young players to get in front of college coaches. Before long, the tournament structure added more venues and tournaments, which gave everybody – the general public included – the opportunity to see the cream of the crop of high school basketball players in their area.

The new blueprint for locating, evaluating and recruiting high school players had arrived. Up until that point, only high level programs used this new system.

Now college programs from all levels used the system for recruiting. This new system changed the game.

Locating prospects to evaluate before Travel Ball was introduced was a challenging process. My recruiting experience began in 1975 at Appalachian State. Back then, the evaluation and recruiting strategies focused on high school games and summer camps. The NCAA had few restrictions on the number of days' coaches could recruit or see players in the off-season.

Popular summer camps like the famed "Five Star Camp" were heavily attended, and almost exclusively regional. If the camp was located in the north, the majority of college coaches doing the evaluating would be from northern schools.

Before 1984, coaches used the high school season as their main channel to evaluate and recruit prospects. Holiday, state and regional tournaments were the only events during the academic year where coaches had the opportunity to see numerous teams play. For the most part, those tournaments only featured sixteen teams. This made finding legitimate college prospects difficult and resulted in many failed recruiting trips.

The high school season was the main source for recruiting. It presented challenges for the college head coach who was immersed in coaching his own team, which resulted in evaluation decisions being made by his staff of assistants. The head coach couldn't be as involved as he wanted and needed to be in on evaluating these high school players, and had to rely heavily on rating services, tapes and tips from high school coaches, alumni, friends and newspaper articles just to get a feel for a player before making the trip to evaluate them.

During this era, a coach might only see fifty college prospects the entire high school season. It was also very common for assistant coaches to miss their own team's games because the recruiting window was small. Add to that both college and high school seasons which were always at the same time.

I made many recruiting trips as a head and assistant coach, spending hours getting to a high school game only to quickly evaluate and learn the player was not good enough, and then having to take the long journey back home.

There was no question that Travel Ball became a great place for coaches to watch hundreds of prospects compete against each other in three-day tournaments. This new era gave college coaching staffs complete control over the evaluation process. No longer having to rely on outside opinions anymore, this structure now gave the head coach the opportunity to evaluate players because these events were outside of the college season.

Key to Remember

- The landscape of how college coaches located prospects completely changed in the mid-80s. Coaches were presented with new ways to evaluate players. This all started with Nike's focus on how to better market their apparel.
- The coaches embraced this opportunity because the old way was more of a struggle in finding prospects to evaluate and recruit. Coaches were now able see more prospects with a better chance of assessing a player's ability while competing against good talent.
- This new method of finding prospects became so popular with the coaches that the NCAA started to consider more oversight in learning how this new structure implemented by outside sources was operating. The NCAA eventually put in rules that limited what Nike and ultimately other apparel companies could do to recruit players to their camps.
- The idea of a sponsored team system was a solid marketing strategy created by the apparel companies. It gave them an effective approach for marketing outreach though the elite players and gave college coaches more and better opportunities to evaluate talent.
- No matter how old a child is who is thinking about playing college basketball, it is important to understand the history of how things were formerly done. The journey to how things are done today has had an impact on kids of all ages, of which many parents and players are not aware.
- The lack of understanding this prior history is the foundation to creating the myths that drive many of the things being done by parents and players today to improve performance, as well as trying to get evaluated by college coaches and making college rosters. Many of the things being done are not getting the results for which parents and players are hoping.

CHAPTER 2

A Spinoff Travel Team Idea is Launched

"Beware of false knowledge; it is more dangerous than ignorance."
- GEORGE BERNARD SHAW

n the early 90's, an influx of tournaments started popping up everywhere which were not sponsored by the apparel companies. The event organizers of these tournaments had no requirements for players on the rosters. This enticed parents and players to recruit local players and organize their own teams. This was the beginning of a Travel Team system that was created as a business opportunity for tournament organizers.

The financial structure of these tournaments was a powerful business model. Using the philosophy of the original Travel Team concept, which included college coaches attending games, these tournaments attracted an incredible number of teams. All this was created from the assumption that college coaches would come. What was missing was the understanding of how college recruiting works.

I was shocked when our business at Suwanee Sports Academy began to rent the facility to tournament organizers. It was eye opening to learn the different revenue sources for these tournaments. It was not just team registrations and spectator fees. They would get a percentage from products sold at the event such as t-shirt screening, team uniforms and personal videos of games, just to name a few. The organizers would also make deals with local hotels, which advertised their facilities as places to stay in return for receiving a stipend for each room sold.

A majority of today's Travel Teams compete in this tournament model created by entrepreneurial organizers, and this new concept created many misconceptions for parents and high school players. They perceived these tournaments were the "real deal." They believed the games were important because the atmosphere had a true feeling of professionalism. The players in uniform, coaches, officials, scorekeepers, clock operators, along with paying spectators was all a façade. I will explain further in upcoming chapters why this perception cannot be related to a true basketball team experience.

This was the beginning of America's youth putting the opportunity to get on a college coach's radar and being evaluated as the priority when playing basketball. What was lost was the understanding that a player needed to spend time and focus on *getting ready* for that evaluation opportunity. As more and more of these teams were formed, it began to change the mindset of high school players. They began to think they were a lot better than they actually were.

The downside was that most parents and players got away from spending valuable time and money on the things necessary to get a good evaluation. They only worried about what they had to do to get evaluated. They were putting the cart before the horse!

I communicate to parents often that the idea of playing multiple games a day is identical to playing many pickup games in a day. The Travel Ball concept is organized pickup games.

As I grew up playing the game, I remember coaches always saying, "You cannot play the game tired or out of shape." This was not all related to only the physical aspect of the game because often the first thing that happens to a player is mental fatigue. The game requires energy, both physical and mental, because of the continuous play going up and down the court. A proper game of basketball was just not designed to be played more than once a day.

When I evaluated players in a tournament environment during my college coaching career, I made sure I saw them play their first game of the day. This was the only way I could get a true assessment of their abilities. This was when they were at full strength, both physically and mentally. I watched additional games that day, but never critiquing their reactions or emotions because I knew they were not at 100%.

Adam Silver, NBA Commissioner made this statement recently about the number of games being played.

"The more we study the wear-and-tear on their bodies, we're now seeing the type of injuries in young players we used to see when they were much older. I think there needs to be more of a holistic response to this. It isn't just about whether the minimum age should be 19 versus 20. I think, as I've said before, we

need to get together with the larger basketball community and talk about the number of games these young players, boys, are playing, beginning 12, 13, 14, often eight games in a weekend at tournaments. For example, I've said before, in Little League, there's a pitch count. And this is a place where historically at least when I got involved in the league, people were telling the NBA to stay out of youth basketball. I think it's clear now we need to be more involved in youth basketball." [1]

The original Travel Team concept was created to market shoes and apparel to the best high school players in the country. The majority of the players were juniors and seniors in high school. By the mid-90's, the tournaments began to grow in team registrations because they expanded the age groups allowed to participate, eventually starting with eight and nine year-old teams.

No one could have predicted "what came next." The sport began to lose its grip. Soon, the fundamental structure of "how to play basketball" would become lost.

The path you choose for your child's introduction into the sport is critical to the experience and success he or she will have playing the game of basketball.

Two stories of players I coached were part of the original Travel Team concept. They were not eligible to play Travel Ball until high school. This enabled them to have a solid foundation of fundamentals development before participating on a travel team.

Dennis Scott (1987) and Kenny Anderson (1989) were the number one players in America coming out of high school. Both were highly skilled in two different categories. Dennis was a great long-range shooter, and Kenny a fabulous ball handler with scoring skills.

I have had the privilege to coach many future NBA players. I can honestly say Dennis and Kenny were very special. They played the game in slow motion. They often saw things develop before they materialized. These instincts led to very good decision making when it came to passing, shooting and dribbling.

They were taught basketball the old-fashioned way: build the right foundation first, skill instruction, acquiring the knowledge to be proficient and understand how to be successful while developing a good work ethic. Their practice habits must have been amazing growing up because when I saw them for the first time it was mind-boggling what they could do.

---

1   RealGm Staff Report, RealGM Wiretap, NBA Continues to Prefer Two Years of College Before Draft Eligibility, basketball.realgm.com

Kenny Anderson is one of the best ball handlers to ever play the game. How he dribbled and passed was extraordinary. It was a daily occurrence for someone to say "did he just do that," or, "he didn't do what I think he did," when watching him practice or play a game.

Dennis, at 6'8," shot effortlessly from long range. He would shoot from half court exactly like he would shoot a foul shot. I often tell a story about Dennis, because it sums up how confident a shooter he was, regarding a game we were playing at Duke.

About an hour before tipoff, the entire student section was full. Their student body was as unique as any in the country. They were always in unison, and totally up to date and knowledgeable about the opponent. Our players were casually shooting around. I happened to be seated in the stands when I saw Dennis talking with the students and telling a few to come out of the stands to shoot. I had no idea what was going on until Dennis explained it to me as he came off the court, getting ready for our pre-game talk.

Dennis challenged five students to take one three point shot each. In return, he would shoot from half court. As I watched this unfold, the Duke students, one at a time, missed all five shots. Dennis then went to half court and with ease swished his shot. As he turned to leave the court, the entire student section responded by bowing with total respect for what they had just witnessed.

If you come through our youth basketball system in America today, you are hard pressed to find a "Dennis or a Kenny" because their introduction into the game has changed. Kids today are getting their skills taught piecemeal from many different sources. There is no continuity in technique. If your child practices on their own, plays travel ball or pickup games, chances are good bad habits are being created.

You can enjoy watching your child having fun playing a sport. Your child might always have a ball in their hands, practicing on their own (which is how kids get better), but the big difference today is the belief that "practice makes perfect." In the past, the mentality was "perfect practice makes perfect."

Basic skills are the building blocks of basketball. Everything on the court depends on the execution of the fundamentals. Proper execution of team skills depend on individual fundamentals, not on how well plays are practiced.

Basketball in America has been negatively impacted from our youth levels all the way to the NBA. Three decades of kids have been introduced to the sport without the proper foundation of instruction on skill technique. They are also missing the importance of learning how to establish a work ethic.

I constantly hear parents making the excuse as to why kids are not as good today as they once were. Their reasoning is that in the past kids grew up playing in the outdoor parks, pickup games and playing half court 3 on 3. But it doesn't matter where and how the games are played that make a players' skills better. The simple answer is that as long as a player has been taught the fundamental skills *correctly*, they will continue to improve no matter where and how they decide to play the game.

Don't assume that staying the course and doing things in the same way as so many others is a player's only choice. Upcoming chapters of this book will give insight into other alternatives and proven formulas which will give your child success on all levels along their basketball journey.

Key to Remember

- As the perception increased that the best way to get on a college coach's radar was to attend youth basketball tournaments, many different tournament operators throughout the United States recognized the *business* opportunity to launch more and more tournaments.
- The influx of all the tournament operators began to mask the original intention for the sponsored team strategy which was to create an evaluation environment for the older, elite kids who college coaches needed for their basketball program rosters.
- As the younger kids and their parents started to look for the edge and follow what the older, elite players were doing, tournament operators launched many tournaments for both the young and older age groups. The tournaments also attracted players of all skill levels, no longer just the elite players.
- The younger kids and parents began to go down a path of playing more games in these tournaments. Their participation did not give them an edge by participating at earlier ages as they thought it would. At the same time, the shift to more games at the younger age groups put more emphasis on playing games, leaving no time or focus for these younger kids to learn the fundamentals and develop their skills needed to play the game. Without a good foundation of skills, a child's success in reaching for their potential will be limited.
- Playing all these games also had a negative impact on an effective evaluation process for college coaches. The players could not sustain their level of play

in all these back-to-back games. Playing more than one game a day caused fatigue to limit players from showing how good they really were. It's unreasonable to expect a child to play well after one game. It is physically impossible because the energy needed to play again, on the same day, was lost in the first game.

Be sure to access bonus content as my gift to you

www.KevinCantwellBasketball.com/p/gifts

SECTION 2

Playing Basketball - How Good Can My Child Really Be?

"You have to learn the rules of the game, and then you have to play better than anyone else."

– ALBERT EINSTEIN

have lived and experienced this section of the book over and over. It is always important before setting a goal to understand the odds of reaching your goal. It could be making a middle school team, a high school team or trying to play college ball. Knowing what you are up against is vital.

The most important thing to understand, even though basketball is a team sport, is that a player will always be judged on their individual skills when trying out for teams. Coaches will run drills with the sole objective of seeing how good a player's skills are. I have listened to both parents and players talk about their hopes for making a team, only to discover that the likelihood of them making it was very unlikely.

Tryouts are a very nerve-wracking time for both parents and kids. You can decrease your worry by finding out from coaches their objective or purpose of the tryout. Basketball is a position sport. Knowing what position your son or daughter plays instantly gives you more knowledge for what the chances are of making a team.

The tryouts I have to help parents understand the most are the ones held before entering high school. They are often your child's first attempt at trying to prove they are better than others. The challenge with these assessments is they are not totally based on talent level alone. Size is also a factor in being chosen for roster spots.

Roster decisions can also be influenced by "politics." The reasons are not related to skills or size. These factors alone have discouraged many kids from believing they are good enough to play basketball. It is important to understand these kinds of decisions, for the most part, do not come into play as kids mature in size. Coaches are held more accountable for their team's performances.

I encourage parents and players to eliminate any doubts a coach might have about a player being chosen for a team roster. Become so good that there is no question choosing your child is the coaches' right decision.

The desire to become the best your child can be will put your child on a journey that will go beyond basketball. The commitment to achieve that goal is so intense that it will be ingrained in your child's character and have a positive impact in every area of his or her life.

CHAPTER 3

Treat Basketball as an Individual Sport

> *"You have to have the work ethic. You have to*
> *push yourself and not be satisfied."*
> – Kobe Bryant

Basketball in the US has completely reversed the formula on how to correctly teach and learn how to play. Regardless of what sport it is, all sports start with individual fundamentals. But we are now the only country in the world putting basketball competition ahead of individual skills.

Basketball is an individual sport when it comes to player development. Any team sport coach may cringe hearing this statement without understanding the meaning of what I am saying. But it's true. Coaches begin to construct their teams on all levels with an initial assessment of each player's individual skills.

Without a fundamental skill base, a player's individual improvement will level off. As the competitive talent gets better, a player will lack the skills to compete.

The perception of younger players and parents is that team wins are the priority, and relying on their teammates has become our approach to a player thinking they are improving. Team wins are the barometer parents and players use to rate individual skills improvement. This is just *not* the case!

The idea that jump shots made in a winning game are signs of improving as a shooter, or that making a good pass shows better passing skills is not realistic. Every game is not the same because every opponent is different, which makes each situation different. Some games and opponents are easier, while others are harder. Good, consistent play is the only way to determine a player's improvement.

More games played will not make players improve and get better. That would be the same as saying that in order to become a good and better golfer, emphasis must be placed on playing as many rounds as possible. The physical action a pro golfer takes in a four-hour round of golf is on average less than two minutes. How can a golfer improve when only working on his swing for two minutes?

The preparation that goes into playing an individual sport like golf is all about training, finding the right resources to train with, and spending quality time preparing for competition. Golfers spend their quality time on the driving range, putting green, and sand traps. I once read that when Tiger Woods made a small change in his swing, he had to hit 10,000 balls to feel comfortable with the change.

Going with the golf analogy, a basketball player would need to create their own "driving range" if they wanted to change weaknesses into strengths and make their strengths even better to prepare for tougher competition. Always remember that your child is going to get evaluated as an individual at every tryout on their journey to make next level teams, so this is a priority.

A similar analogy can be used for individuals playing a game of basketball. If a player plays every minute of a high school game, 32 minutes, you will touch the ball on average two minutes. If you play a 20 game season and play every minute, you will touch the ball for 40 minutes over the entire season. If you are able to play every minute over four years, 80 games, you will touch the ball for two hours and 40 minutes.

The question should be about how good are players when they have the ball? This is why I say it is an individual sport. What is being done to build up your child's strengths to a greater level? How are they working to improve their weaknesses? When competing and striving to win, it is human nature to do what is done best and feels "natural." Are players always using their strengths? When and how do players work to improve on what they don't do well? How much time is your child working on those skills? A player cannot improve his or her skills by simply playing the game. It is impossible.

One defining characteristic of every successful athlete is that they practiced long hours for many years to develop their competitive edge. A player will never get to the stage where they have practiced enough. Vince Lombardi once said, "The harder you work, the harder it is to surrender."

Key to Remember

- While basketball is a team game, a player will always be evaluated on their individual skills. No matter what team a player is trying out for, the coach's initial decision when choosing the players for his team will all be based on individual talent.
- To understand the mentality for how a player is to approach the individual aspect of working on their skills, it is similar to a golfer spending hours on the driving range. Repetitions of working on a skill are the only way to improve while just playing the game will not give a player this opportunity. The simple fact that the amount of time the ball is touched during a game supports why individual training is mandatory for continued improvement.
- A critical piece to a player working on their own is to make certain that they have been taught the correct technique in shooting and dribbling. Without this crucial piece they will be spending their time practicing on skills the wrong way.
- Our youth believe they are doing what it takes to improve because of the amount of time they spend playing basketball, but that is *quantity* time. The missing piece is a player working by themselves, spending *quality* time improving as an individual.
- Finding the right balance between playing games and individual development is a necessity. The majority of the time needs to be spent on individual development.

CHAPTER 4

Desire and Discipline = Quantity and Quality Learning

"In reading the lives of great men, I found that the
first victory they won was over themselves.
Self-discipline with all of them came first."
— HARRY S. TRUMAN

An important and relevant question a player needs to ask themselves if they have the desire to become as good as they can be; how long is a long enough time to practice? The truth is that it's not ability that stops players from moving up the ladder, but rather it is the lack of drive to train and practice more than the majority. But the key is to train and practice on the right things! Remember, perfect practice makes perfect. Ensure your child's time is being well spent.

The only way to become a potential college basketball player is to work harder than everybody else on the right things. It is very important for the player to constantly be reminded of this objective. We live in the moment which too often takes us away from seeing the big picture.

This is why it is so critical for young players to improve their skills in the off-season. More than anything else, the need is to control the quantity time being spent on team practices and games in relation to the quality time spent training on their improvement. This has become challenging because there is very little, or no, off-season left in youth basketball.

Manage the balance between playing games and training to learn how to play. If a player has any questions about what the right balance is, he or she can't go wrong with overemphasizing the training to learn how to play the game. The only way to gain respect from peers and to catch the eye of coaches is to show constant improvement in a player's individual skills.

The belief that Travel Ball participation is the number one way to improve drives the thinking that it is important to start playing at an early age. Early age participation starts the downward spiral because it places a major emphasis on playing games rather than learning *how* to play the game.

This gives parents and players false hope thinking that all the hours of playing games and team practice to prepare for those games is laying the foundation for their child to get better and be the best they can be. They are thinking this is putting them on the right path to becoming successful, when in fact, it is putting them on the wrong path.

There is a time and place for games. They have become a key part of the US youth basketball system. But you must be more aware of how all the game participation benefits a player and how it doesn't. Kobe Bryant grew up in Italy. He was asked what type of player he would be if he grew up in America. He said, "I probably wouldn't be able to dribble with my left hand or shoot with my left, or have good footwork."

Choosing teams and getting ready for the Travel Team season is an annual process and has become a tradition in our youth basketball world. This thinking is driving the belief that being in this system at an early age is mandatory to being successful. This begins the obsession for parents believing playing in tournaments and the excitement surrounding competition is the best way for their child to become an effective player.

In reality this misconception is the beginning of getting on the wrong path for how to become a good player. It is critical for parents to understand the negativity of making competition the main focus too early in a child's basketball journey. Also, recognize that playing all these games will not prepare them for the point in time when getting on a college coach's radar and getting evaluated becomes important.

Another key factor involving too much competition that gets completely overlooked is how it leads to low self-esteem. Competition, for the most part, beats a player down. The main focus is on their mistakes. This makes players feel like they have to be perfect. No matter how good a player is, constant competition will take away confidence because it is impossible to play the game perfectly. With all the responsibilities that are required of a player, they inherently are put into situations to fail.

I spent 28 years as a college coach. After playing a 30 game schedule, our players and staff needed the seven-month off-season to regroup mentally and get our confidence back. It is not mentally healthy to put your child in the position to play three to five games in a weekend tournament.

Labeling Kids Too Early

Lacking the proper skills to perform well in games at an early age also puts a player in a position to be labeled immediately by youth coaches. Taller kids are told to stay off the perimeter and play inside. Only certain kids are allowed to shoot and dribble. Developing all the fundamental skills for ALL players at an early age is so important because as a player gets older, he or she will be capable of playing multiple positions.

This type of labeling reduces the learning process for kids. It is the beginning of poor basketball skill development in many of the fundamental areas of the game required for success as they get older. There is such false hope as I watch kids succeed for all sorts of reasons at early ages. Their success so often has very little to do with skills. Eventually those attributes are nullified when other kids catch up to them. When the individual skills are needed, it is so often too late. They are not good enough. It doesn't have to end up that way!

Early success is usually due to height and physical maturity. These attributes will slowly become a non-factor for roster spots because skill, speed and athleticism begin to be the criteria as the kids get older. As a player's skills improve, confidence grows. And feeling good about yourself is so important in anything we do and strive to excel at in life.

Keep Focus On Big Picture. Only So Much Time – Use It Wisely

Competing at an early age is enjoyable to watch as your child learns the rules and movements of the game but he is losing valuable time in actually becoming a good basketball player. The right balance of playing games and learning to play the game is so important at all ages, but especially the younger ages.

Too much time being spent on team practices, travel and playing in tournaments that often create game schedules of 60 to100 games is not the best use of time and money if the goal is to discover just how good your child can be playing basketball.

Parents and players get caught up in the weekend tournament hoopla. Don't get blindsided by the competitive environment and forget what is the big picture. To find out just how good your child can be at the sport of basketball, the priority needs to be focused on becoming individually skilled through a player development program. This will also make participation in the sport more fun. Kids always have more fun when they feel successful at what they are doing.

If your child truly wants to make any team at the next level of youth basketball, if they want to one-day play college basketball, the solid foundation of individual skill development will make them a legitimate college prospect. They will then be ready for the time when it is important to be working on exposure to college coaches and getting evaluated for the recruiting process.

Making a Basketball Commitment!

I don't want parents to perceive that I am trying to tell them it is not a great experience for kids to play different sports. Playing other sports can be fun. Playing different sports can help kids find the sport they are meant to play. This decision to focus on one sport needs to be made by their freshman year in high school at the latest.

I want parents to understand that if it is their child's goal is to play college basketball, the earlier they dedicate and specialize their focus to the sport of basketball, the better their chances are to reach that goal. The stories about multisport athletes are true, but they are not an everyday occurrence.

To achieve your child's dream of playing college basketball, he or she must give themselves an edge to compete against everybody else who has that same dream. This edge will come from spending as much time as possible developing their basketball skills.

I often hear people say other sports will prepare a player to be a better basketball player. I just don't believe that is true. Basketball is one of the only sports where players go from offense to defense in a split second. I have always stressed that *skills* are the most important aspect needed to become a good player. Taking time off to play another sport slows down a player's progress.

Soccer is one of the sports people compare to basketball. They perceive it offers great conditioning and can help improve footwork. The problem, though, is that in soccer the ball cannot be touched. Ball handling in basketball is the most important skill needed!

Footwork and ball handling must be learned together. One cannot be worked on without the other. Ball handling is not just dribbling. It is hand coordination and fingertip control when catching, passing, shooting and rebounding, all performed in a small area. No other sport can help improve what is required in basketball.

Splitting time with another sport just makes the dream even more difficult when trying to become the best you can be as well as considering the odds of playing in college. The time spent honing in on a player's individual skills will take them to another level. When the time comes to be evaluated, they will be ready to impress coaches at any level leading up to college basketball.

Don't put your child in a position where they end up saying, "I wish I had spent more time developing my skills" when you have learned what is really important to a college coach's recruiting decisions. It will be too late to do anything about it at that point.

A player can never perfect their skills. What is needed is to take the time they have and get them to the highest level possible. Thinking they are good enough and can take time off from working on their skills is an inaccurate assumption if your child wants to achieve their goal of being the best they can be.

As a parent, the need is to start your children early, have a plan for their development, get the right resources to help, and focus as much time as possible on getting them to become better and better.

Love The Game. Become the Best You Can Be

All players should strive to become the best they can be. This has to be their mentality. If they focus only on winning and losing at too early an age, they will never find out just how good they can be. This will cause them to only like the game instead of loving the game. Loving the game means putting in countless hours working on developing individual skills. A player can't find the drive or internal motivation to work hard without a real love of the game.

The majority of youth basketball players only like the game because the focus overemphasizes playing games. Being really good at something requires the discipline to work on the things that sometimes aren't as fun as other things. A player has to love the game to really find out how good they can be.

If their goal is to become the best they can be and to play college basketball, it is critical to have clarity on what they need to do to make that goal a reality. Understanding the approach and commitment needed for training and development will give them the mindset of loving basketball instead of just liking it. This will provide them the dedication and commitment required to succeed.

The Key to Success - Quality Time versus Quantity Time

It will be impossible for a player to reach their goals of making the team at the next level without a solid commitment to do the right things needed, and when to do them. The player's individual player development program commitment will require him or her to not play so many games in the off-season. Remember the importance of quality time spent versus quantity time spent.

Skill development is the quality time players need to spend to get better. There is a time for playing games for fun as well as development. The right mix of one versus the other is critical to the success of any player becoming as good as they can be.

Players have to believe beyond any doubt that their approach will be the only way to get on any coach's radar at any level of play. Emulating habits of successful players is usually the motivator to get this type of mindset, but initially they may stand alone because the perception in America to "become the best you can become" is to play as many games as possible in competitive tournaments in the off-season. Players need to believe in their quality time commitment for improving their individual skills.

A player documents their approach and is focused on the mission of becoming the best they can be by working on their own. Discipline will be needed in making this mission successful. It will require many hours of time alone training. Players will have to manage all of the areas needed in their player development program and locate experts in these areas of skills training as well as speed, quickness and strength training. The training time allocated to a player's development program will be their decision, but remember, there is no special or set number of minutes required. The more quality time put in, the better the player will become.

Making individual workouts a priority will be a very mature decision compared to the approach of other players and friends. The majority of people will see more games and more competition as the best approach to getting better, but when they recognize this approach is not the right one, it is too late to do anything about it. Do everything you can to ensure you and your child have no regrets about their basketball journey. You don't want to find yourself wishing you had done things differently.

I had the incredible opportunity during my college coaching career to recruit the best players in America. I was able to listen and observe how the best made it. For the most part they all had so much pride which made them getting better an obsession. They were obsessed with working on their individual skills on their own.

Key to Remember

- Don't put playing the game as the priority in developing your child's basketball talent. It is not the way to begin this journey. Getting caught up in the action and competition at such an early age will slow the developmental process.

- Thinking your child's basketball resume needs to have so many years playing Travel Ball has no value when it comes to being the best you can be. College coaches evaluate talent, not the number of years playing youth basketball.
- Playing games will not make your child better. Even more importantly, it is not good for their self-esteem. Competition mentally beats you up. Playing numerous games in one day often becomes demoralizing.
- The most important part of the journey for getting on a coach's radar is when the time comes for evaluation. Your child must be ready talent-wise for the evaluation. The objective is not to get evaluated. It is to be *ready* for the evaluation when the time comes.
- Playing more than one sport is important early on just to see which sport your child enjoys more. The longer it takes to make a decision on which sport to focus on, the less chance of becoming the best they can be at that sport.
- Basketball is unique. It is the only sport that goes from offense to defense in a split second. It is a sport which requires constant concentration and individual skills that will always need improvement. Dedicated focus to train and practice on a player's own is critical to success.
- To become the best a player can become, they have to have a love for the game. The majority of kids in America like basketball. They put a lot of time into it, but it is quantity time spent playing in weekend tournaments. Spending seven to eight months playing games is quantity time.
- The shift has to move to *quality* time, which is an individual devotion to getting better. This becomes a real love for the game, locating the right resources to assist in their development, spending the majority of their time by themselves training with lots of repetitions. Taking pride in themselves to always strive to improve will make them the best they can become. It will bring out their real love for the game.
- The most damaging aspect of playing so many off-season games is that players today are not learning to play the game, and therefore, aren't really preparing to be evaluated by coaches. What has been forgotten is the understanding of how to become the best a player can be. The overemphasis for getting on a coach's radar has taken the place of preparing to show your best once you get on that radar.

CHAPTER 5

Basketball IQ – Knowing Your Role – Scoring Points Overrated

"Absorb what is useful, discard what is not,
add what is uniquely your own."
– BRUCE LEE

A player with great knowledge of the game often is referred to as someone with a high "basketball IQ." Knowing how to play the game comes from a dedication to working on the right things for a long time.

During the course of playing too many games when participating in the US grass-roots basketball system, things such as poor shooting, turnovers and a lack of defense are often not frowned upon because players have to get ready to play the next game.

In an organized setting, the game of basketball was never designed to be played more than one game a day. To play the game correctly, mentally and physically, players need to avoid being tired. Fatigue creates more missed shots, turnovers and poor defense.

Basketball IQ and what to do when a player does not have the ball are the real drivers of finding out just how good a player can be. Today's players are obsessed with scoring points; this is driven by the Travel Ball system mentality of playing so many games. If you ask players how they played, ninety percent of them will gauge their performances on the number of points they did or did not score.

But points are overrated. When analyzing a player's performance, this is not the most essential factor. But this thinking has caused the sport of basketball in the US to lose focus on what is important.

It takes two seconds to take a shot. If you played 25 minutes in a game and took 15 shots, that is two seconds times 15 shots equaling 30 seconds spent shooting the basketball. That means for 24 minutes and 30 seconds you are performing other important aspects of the game. Points are overrated!

Know Your Role

Knowing a player's role is the most important way to become an effective player. Understanding a player's strengths and weaknesses in all aspects of the game are crucial to how he or she will perform.

If a player is not tall, their role as a rebounder should be to box out. If their lateral movement is weak, then their role as a defender is not to take chances. If they are not explosive with the ball than don't drive to the basket.

Kids today do not understand the concept of role. They play the game thinking they can do anything they want to do including taking shots that have very little chance of going in. But when it does go in they believe it was a result of their good decision.

Understanding the different roles that describe players is very important. A player cannot have the mentality that they are capable of doing everything. Quickly defining their role as a player is necessary to continue to improving as a player.

Offensive efficiency has taken a back seat to everyone thinking they can do it all. This leads to out of control basketball and poor shooting. Scoring points can be achieved in many ways. Layups, jump shots, 2 pointers or 3's, foul shots, back to basket moves, offensive put backs and taps. It is crucial to understand the most efficient way a player can score points because without that knowledge they will constantly put themselves in the position to play poorly.

Scorer versus Shooter

When I was evaluating players, there were two labels I would use to describe them; a scorer or shooter.

1. Shooter – a player capable of shooting open jump shots at a high percentage; able to make a majority of 3 pointers.
2. Scorer – usually the more athletic player, and can score in different ways. Very explosive creating his or her own shot, getting fouled, offensive rebounder.

The majority of kids today don't understand their strengths and weaknesses, so they play to both definitions. As a result, their offensive game doesn't fit either description. Most kids want to be scorers because to make these moves they have to be creative and constantly driving toward the basket. The problem is only the true scorers know how to avoid turnovers and put the ball in the basket 45% of the time.

Being a scorer-type player is just not possible for everyone. All players don't fit the definition. This is what makes Travel Ball a challenge for players who don't have the scorer skill sets. The fast style of play forces players into making creative moves that many are not really capable of making.

The label of being a shooter is possible for everyone. Scorers need special physical attributes but shooters are decided on the skill only. It is very important to understand just because a player can make shots does not label them a shooter. To gain this description they have to shoot at a high percentage and make clutch shots. The most convincing factor is a coach's perception of a shooter having the correct form.

Very few American youth players today own the title of being a shooter. Our college game is desperate for players with this ability. With such a shortage of shooters at every level of the game today, why wouldn't you as a parent focus your son or daughter on building this skill? It is a great opportunity for playing at the next level.

Along with being able to effectively score points, shooters are invaluable players in a number of ways. For example, they cannot be left unguarded. Their ability to force double teams leaves other players open. They can force a defense to spread out and provide more opportunity for teammates who are scorers.

When evaluating players, coaches always envision how a shooter would perform in their system. Shooters are viewed as players who are valuable if surrounded by good players. If a team has a good inside game with shooters on the perimeter, their offense is almost unstoppable.

If your son or daughter does not fit the definition of an athlete, then the only offensive asset he or she can possess to get the attention of coaches at any level is to be labeled a shooter.

Every player needs to have a good knowledge of the game in order to clearly understand his or her role. When he or she has clarity and buy-in for their role along with understanding their strengths and weaknesses, they can focus on the many things required to be the best player he or she can be. This will then put them in the best position to be wanted by coaches at any level of play throughout their years of playing the game.

Key to Remember

- The Travel Ball system has taught me what happens to a player's individual mentality when playing so many games a day and not having efficient time to practice. The attention to detail on individual performance gets totally lost because coaches lack the time to define player roles. The end results are players believe they can make offensive moves they are not capable of making.
- Scoring points has now become the statistic that defines how kids play. This leads to players not worrying about shooting percentages. Coaches lack the time to teach all phases of the game during team practice. Teaching our youth how to play the game has been lost.
- Scoring points can be achieved in many ways. Layups, jump shots, 2 pointers or 3's, foul shots, back to basket moves, offensive put backs and taps.
- One phase of the game that has lacked guidance is the concept of offensive efficiency. When it comes to offensive scoring, a player is either a scorer or a shooter. Scorers are athletic and can make jump shots but have the ability to score points in other ways by creating their own shot. Shooters are players making jump shots at a high percentage.
- It is so important for players to understand their capabilities. This helps them stay away from bad performances. The majority of kids today do not fit the scorer's definition but, without guidance, they take on this role.
- The Travel Team style of play leans heavily towards creativity when trying to score points. Players who are legitimate scorers are hard to come by. Many of our American youth players believe they fit both roles of scorers and shooters. Watching kids take shots they are not capable of making is the norm when watching many American youth players.
- Our youth don't take on a shooters' mentality because the Travel Ball style of play is more about creating their own shot driving to the basket. Very little attention is put on how to shoot properly because no emphasis is placed on teaching the proper shooting mechanics.

CHAPTER 6

What Kind of Player Should You Be? Emulate the International Player

"It's better to hang out with people better than you. Pick out associates whose behavior is better than yours and you'll drift in that direction."
— WARREN BUFFETT

The number of highly skilled players in America are at a minimum. The mentality to put playing the game above skill development is the main reason for the major influx of players from overseas to the US. The international player development concept puts skill development as the priority. During the off-season, international players work on their development. Plain and simple, this is why these players continue to take roster spots at the highest basketball levels in the US.

Their approach to player development is nothing new. This mentality was once how American kids learned the game because there was an off-season that was strictly dedicated to getting better.

Many international players attend basketball academies that last up to six months every year. The curriculum is teaching how to play basketball. They learn early on the first step to becoming successful is their individual skill set with an intense emphasis on footwork, ball-handling and shooting.

Their instructors are certified and accountable for each player's actions and performance. The objective is to develop good players who can represent their country in the different age brackets as they grow through their systems.

I have spent the last 15 years studying, learning and observing a completely different fundamental approach being taught to international players. It has become obvious to me American coaches/instructors have missed this dramatic change that should have been adopted here in the US. The reason is due to the fact that US youth basketball has focused for close to 30 years now on playing games and not staying in tune to new philosophies regarding individual skill improvement.

An international instructor that fascinated me was Dirk Nowitzki's teacher, Holger Geschwindner from Germany. He studied math and physics and considers himself the "Einstein of Basketball." He applies that mentality in his teaching. His business card has his picture on it with an Einstein hairdo.

The name of his company is "Institute of Applied Nonsense." This title came about when he started training Dirk because all the methods he used were considered plain nonsense. His philosophy turned Dirk into a great basketball player.

Geschwindner is an unbelievable instructor when teaching the skills of footwork, ball-handling and shooting. He helps players perform these skills with precision and quickness. The area of his philosophy that was questioned by many was his physics and math background applied to body movement. Teaching how to make all individual movements equally, dealing with the lower body and the effectiveness it can have on a player's performance.

I personally use this method in training. No matter what drill I am working on, the point of emphasis is always on teaching how the lower body dictates efficient movement. Because this ideology doesn't exist here in the US, I get the same response Holger received when he introduced his philosophy. I have had college coaches tell me it is too hard to teach, there isn't enough time to teach it and some just don't get it.

This method is not hard to incorporate into any coach's teaching philosophy and methodologies. It also doesn't have to be too time consuming to teach. It can be taught as part of any of the drills coaches are already working on with their players. It just needs to become a point of emphasis. The understanding of this innovative technique has been adopted by international coaches and players. It has been proven to be extremely effective as these players continue to be successful playing in college and the NBA.

Knowing how effective this method is can improve anyone's ability. It is often frustrating watching kids play knowing that they could take their talent to higher levels if they had this knowledge of the importance of equal body movement.

An international player committed to a basketball way of life is a hard combination to beat. If your son or daughter really wants to find out how good they can be, and one-day play college basketball, he or she should emulate how the international players commit themselves to their craft. This approach will provide the competitive edge when the time comes to perform in games.

Kobe Bryant has spoken out on our youth basketball system using words like, "horrible," "terrible," and, "stupid," saying the system doesn't teach our kids to play the game. He believes European players are more skillful than American players and it is a growing trend. He says, "They are taught the game the right way at an early age... they're more skillful, it is something we really have to fix."

What Type of Player is Your Son or Daughter?

A player can help beat the odds and be good enough to play college basketball as soon as they understand the type of player they are. If they are not cut out of the athletic mold, they must work even harder to perfect their skills. They can still beat the odds! But trust me when I say, they will NOT beat the odds by just playing games.

The majority of American players being recruited to play college ball are athletes who are not very offensively skilled, but they can assist in other areas of the game such as defense and rebounding.

Basketball isn't a game where you can just show up, and by just doing that alone you will become good. It's a very challenging game. There's no substitute for getting good instruction in all aspects of the game and practicing a lot. That is the only way. It's okay to just show up and play if a player is only interested in having fun. But if they want to get better, they have to work their butts off on the right things.

Highly skilled U.S. players are becoming a rare breed at all ages. If your child wants to find the edge and impress coaches, concentrate on building individual talent. The most important thing is to never stop working on getting better. Remember there is always somebody working harder!

Key to Remember

- The biggest misfortune for American youth basketball is that our coaches/instructors have not kept up with teaching new ways to develop our US players. This has enabled the international players to take over the skill position spots on college and pro teams in the United States.

- The majority of kids lack basketball athleticism, but that does not mean a player cannot compete against athletic-type players. The attention to developing individual skills has to be a priority.
- What international players are doing to develop their individual skills is identical to how American kids once worked to improve their skills before the big emphasis in the US became playing more and more games.

Be sure to access bonus content as my gift to you

www.KevinCantwellBasketball.com/p/gifts

SECTION 3

Keys to Individual Skill Development

"I don't focus on what I am up against. I focus on my goals and try to ignore the rest."
— Venus Williams

T his section gives the basketball solutions which determine how your child can accomplish his or her goals. It provides an in-depth look at the key aspects of player development with a personal formula he or she can follow.

My intent with this chapter is NOT to overwhelm you with the details that turn you into a coach so you can teach your child all the important fundamentals of the game. My goal is to provide you with a solid foundation of knowledge so you can understand what is most important for your child to improve as a player. Then, my goal will be to enable you to identify the right player development instructor in your local community who will work best for your child. My teaching philosophy is about getting every player to become the best they can be and helping them play at each level throughout their basketball journey.

I strongly believe anyone can become a successful basketball player with the proper knowledge of what to do and how to do it. Throughout this section I will give you a breakdown of the required individual basketball skills and explain why they are crucial. I also explain how everything can be done.

CHAPTER 7

Parents Beware - An Obstacle to Individual Improvement

"Where there is shouting there is no true knowledge."
– Leonardo da Vinci

have watched hundreds of youth games. And what really gets my attention is seeing how parents watch their kids play. They coach them as spectators from the sidelines. This can actually slow down the learning process of a child.

I listen to parents shouting out the different basketball terminologies as they watch their child play. It is done very innocently. Parents routinely yell, "rebound," "pass," "dribble," "shot," "play defense," whatever they think the situation calls for. It was very obvious to me that they had never coached before. If they had coached, they would realize how hard it is for players to stay focused on individual responsibilities during game play.

I tell parents that what they are trying to communicate to their kids during play for the most part is correct. But it is not realistic to expect their child to follow those commands. It takes years of experience to process an adjustment.

Let's take rebounding as an example. Most kids will shy away from the idea of getting pushed around or making contact with others. You are asking them to be aggressive and to play tough, which takes time to teach.

Rebounding is required at a time during the game when a player's mind is occupied with other responsibilities on the court. For them to immediately change their mindset to focus on rebounding is not as easy as one might perceive. Shouting at them during the game or coaching your child after the game in the area of rebounding is only going to put more pressure on them, and will not help the situation.

Rebounding is one of the hardest skills to teach, even at the college level. We had high school All Americans who had to be reminded constantly. There are two parts to rebounding. First, going to the basket on shots. Next, learning the proper technique so the chances of getting the ball are improved. It took time before they did it instinctively.

Basketball is a game like no other for an individual player. Changing from a defensive role to being on offense in a split second is mentally challenging. There are so many aspects of the game for which everyone is responsible. Players have an offensive position and are assigned a player to defend, but in the flow of a game their duties go way beyond specific assignments.

In my entire coaching career there was one drill that we did consistently. It was a transition drill. It was very simple but extremely hard trying to get all five players to execute properly. The difficult part for the players was transitioning from offense to defense.

It was a 5 on 5 drill. The offensive team ran our offense. On a command, whoever had the ball gave it to his defender who took off on a fast break. This was a physical drill but the main objective was teaching players how to change their focus because they had to quickly transition from offense to defense and defense to offense.

The concentration a player needs to transition their mind from one responsibility to another is identical to working on a skill. It is a learning process and it has to become a habit. College coaches would prefer not to play young kids for this reason. Their lack of concentration causes them to struggle transitioning from one responsibility to another.

Early on in my coaching career I realized a very important coaching lesson that taught me to be patient with younger players. These players, no matter how good their skills were, all lacked the mental concentration to stay focused on their responsibilities when playing. Their minds had to be trained to stay alert and the only method to accomplish this was playing time. When a player accomplishes this task they are then considered to have experience.

One example of this came when we were preparing to play North Carolina State. There best player was Rodney Monroe and we were trying to decide who should guard him. Our choices were only two players: our leading scorer, Jon Barry, or Brian Hill, who was in his first year but physically built for the assignment. We decided on Brian because we did not want Jon wearing himself out, knowing it would affect his offensive performance.

We learned quickly that Brian was not up for this tough responsibility. He was struggling to stay focused when Rodney did not have the ball. He let him repeatedly use screens to get open jump shots. As Brian was given tough defensive assignments in small doses he slowly became a very good defender.

Everyone has to do everything at some point during a game, whether it is shooting, dribbling, passing, rebounding or defending. All these responsibilities have to be taught. This is difficult enough, and without structure in the learning process, a player will never reach their potential.

Coaching from the sideline is distracting. Your child knows your voice and your instructions are discouraging because they cannot do all that you are asking. It works against building their confidence.

Coaches also have to yell instructions from the sidelines during games and practice, so I am very aware of the negative effects this can have on your child. The difference is that we understand at the time what our individual player's capabilities are, so we limit what we expect them to do.

Key to Remember

- For the most part, parents attending their child's basketball game understand the rules and terminology that go along with a player's responsibilities. What is evident when I listen to parents repeatedly yelling instructions to their child during games is they don't have coaching experience and/or have forgotten how tough it is to perform those tasks.
- Basketball is a game that is constantly moving and the player's responsibilities are changing in split seconds. Changing focus is a skill that has to be taught, which takes practice and time.
- The innocent coaching you do from the sideline while watching your child's basketball game can be harmful. Your child wants to do what you say but their minds can't translate it into action. This automatically makes them think negatively about themselves because they cannot do what you are asking.

- Understanding how difficult it is to perform basketball skills both physically and mentally is so important to your child's confidence.
- Remember, the skills that need to be learned are challenging because your child's mind has to instinctively transfer focus from one responsibility to the next.

CHAPTER 8

The Secret Ingredient for Individual Skill Development

"Risk comes from not knowing what you are doing."
– Warren Buffet

As I created my individual training philosophy, I was very conscious of how I got a player to improve as quickly as possible. It took years of experience before I realized that no matter the age or grade level of a player, it was critical to begin with the right foundation.

We are in a new era of fundamentals created outside of the United States. This new era has been adopted by the international basketball communities but, for the most part, ignored in America. If you are looking for an edge to compete on a high level, train your body to be equally coordinated. I have yet to observe an instructor, trainer, volunteer coach or school coach on our grassroots level emphasizing and teaching this skill.

I have spent more than 15 years as a player development instructor and have created my own philosophy by studying the international way of gaining the performance edge which has been proven to be successful. There are two components to making this method work. First, having the complete knowledge of the training philosophy. Second, the method requires an incredible work ethic to train your body movements to be equal.

Coordinating the body to work equally from both sides is the foundation. It is what has been lacking with player development in the US. Body coordination is one of the pillars for the development of an international player. It is the secret ingredient that provides the key to your child making real strides in their skill development

The biggest area of focus should be your child's body movement. Players constantly move in a small area on the court in all directions with nine other people of different sizes and speeds. Just think about the majority of the time your child is playing. It is done without the ball and constantly moving using his or her feet to adjust to different situations.

This philosophy of coordinating the body will address all phases of your child's game. Just concentrating on the normal skills of shooting and dribbling would leave out developing the most important part of a player's game which is learning to move more freely on the court and to be able to physically address any aspect of the game needed at any moment.

The coordination and strength of your lower body is the most important ingredient to becoming an above average player in any sport. Without it you cannot excel. I once read an article on what NFL quarterbacks concentrate on when working in the off-season. Their main focus is on lower body, core hips down to feet because that is where the accuracy and strength of the pass comes from.

Basketball Quickness

Have you ever heard someone describe a player's speed as quick? Being quick has nothing to do with speed or slowness. I have often heard people say there is only so much anyone can do to improve the speed or quickness with which they were born. I disagree!

I agree speed can be hard to improve. Being fast is not a critical asset to becoming a good player because a college court is only 94 feet long, and the majority of the game is played from 28 feet and within.

Regardless of size or speed, players can become basketball "quick." Players can learn how to become quicker, and use it to compete at levels not typically expected. Today's focus on learning how to compete in basketball has been distorted with the belief that a player has to be big and fast to succeed. That is absolutely not true because there are players in college and the NBA who do not have those qualities, but are still very effective.

Quickness starts with body control. I have spent my lifetime recruiting and developing players at the Division I level. Since my recruiting and coaching years at Georgia Tech, competing in the ACC, I have worked with many elementary school, middle school, high school, college and professional players. Everyone is searching for the edge.

I continue to talk with parents and players all the time about how body control is the foundation to improving individual skill development. It is the most important skill that needs to be taught at early ages to achieve the edge. Yet no one ever mentions it. It is so often ignored. Trust me. It is the formula for a player to get better.

A player cannot become a quick shooter or an effective ball handler without having the ability to use BOTH feet equally because that is where the initial body movement happens in order to achieve quickness.

Body Balance is Everything ---- It All Starts with Your Feet

Being quick is the ability to react and change body position at any point in time while in motion, along with being able to run as fast as a player can and having the ability to stop immediately.

Quickness is all about your first and second step moving immediately without delay. A good example to consider is that the fastest person in the world is the Olympic 100-meter winner. Where does his competitive edge come from? He gets it from his quickness out of the blocks, his first and second step.

Kenny Anderson, one of the greatest players ever to come out of New York City, used his quickness as good as anyone I have ever seen play. Offensively Kenny would dribble at his defender. He would freeze him for a split second and then quickly make a successful move. The initial movement giving Kenny his quickness was his feet. Being able to pivot on either foot along with incredible dribbling skills made most of his moves seem effortless.

I can remember so many times in practice watching Kenny move with the ball. In a blink of an eye he either created a shooting situation for himself or the move allowed a teammate to free up. He did things so quickly you were not ready for his end result.

Kenny was a very unique player because his body makeup was not what you would think the second pick in the draft should look like. He was 6"2', not very muscular, had small hands and could barely dunk.

He relied on quickness when dribbling, shooting and rebounding. His dribbling was done with authority, always getting the ball to the floor and back into his hand with amazing quickness. He could shoot with defenders on him, using his feet to stop quickly to take the shot and surprising his defenders. He was considered one of the best rebounding guards in the country because he was always using his quick feet to box out.

Kenny Anderson's formula for attaining his quickness can be achieved by anyone. He was taught the proper fundamentals of dribbling and shooting at an early age. He was taught knowing his feet and legs were needed to effectively assist in all aspects of the game and embraced the concept of individual skill development. Without his belief in individual skill development and work ethic, all his knowledge was worthless.

Anyone can achieve quickness! Each sport has its own individual components of performing actions quickly, and in basketball there are numerous ways to show this. The key body parts needed to focus on to attain quickness are a player's feet. Players cannot become quick shooters, effective dribblers, accurate passers or solid defenders without having both feet coordinated equally.

So many mistakes and turnovers in today's game of basketball are misdiagnosed as poor decisions. I believe the root cause for many of the bad decisions being made are due to poor footwork and body control. Often it is not the decision that caused the turnover but a player being put in a position where they lose control of their body movements which forces the turnover.

Embracing the concept of "body balance" to gain quickness is the formula, the real edge for high performance at any level. Simply put, this means players are able to use their right and left foot equally along with being able to use their right and left hand, equally.

International players in the NBA are not categorized as athletic players, but are competing against great athletic players who are bigger and faster. The common denominator they all exhibit is body balance. This leads to being able to move efficiently and quickly with or without the ball.

Formulating ways to compete are essential. Players must understand how their lower body works. Teaching basketball quickness is the foundation for every skill I teach players. Regardless of the skill; shooting, dribbling or passing. Performing them quickly is the goal.

Right Leg/Foot Dominance versus Left Leg/Foot Dominance

Many people know the importance of being able to use both hands equally when dribbling, passing or shooting a layup. What has been neglected in the development of players at all levels is the importance of using both feet as a competitive edge.

If players practice using their weak hand so they will feel confident when playing, but neglect to coordinate their weak leg, they will still be one dimensional when moving, using their coordinated foot the majority of the time

Your child's skill development should be more dependent on their feet, as much, if not more than any other skill they can learn. The first thing to understand is that we all have a dominant foot. We can always identify a person's dominant hand. We are either right or left-handed. What is not understood is that a person's strong hand dictates their dominant foot.

Right handers have left leg/foot dominance. Left handers have right leg/foot dominance. Foot dominance means the foot that has the most strength when pushing off to move, and is the one that leads the majority of the time when stopping or turning.

I had this ongoing discussion with my son-in-law, a former collegiate soccer player. When I told him his dominant leg was his left because he is "righty," he questioned that because he leads with his right foot when striking a ball to score. Not knowing much about soccer outside of my enjoyment watching the game, I could not articulate a reason why he was wrong.

Finally, after watching many matches during the World Cup, I realized a player might strike the ball with the right foot but all the strength and direction is coming from his dominant leg, his left. After explaining this to him he then realized what I was saying and verified how his left leg does control his striking movement.

A person's dominant leg/foot also leads to another movement that is natural. The direction turned is the result of a person's dominant side. The foot is used as a pivot in order to turn the upper body. A right-handed person will turn to their left because in order to perform the turn naturally they would pivot on their left foot. This example tells the story about quickness! What if the basketball situation required a player to turn to their right? The pivotal point (no pun intended) determines how effectively the player will be able to do that.

Another basketball movement that has to be taught while coordinating the lower body is learning how to perform a "back pivot" using both feet. Back turns are not natural because this type of movement is not used in everyday life. But they are crucial turns in achieving quickness.

Using a back pivot to box out when rebounding is the proper technique to use when teaching a player to rebound, especially if they are oversized. I have noticed over the years that coaches don't teach back pivoting anymore, but still demand their players to rebound well. This is very hard to do if a player doesn't know how to back pivot.

I continue to be a student of the game. Knowing quickness is taught and performed, it so enjoyable to watch. I respect players with this ability because I understand the work that goes into developing their bodies to move so fluidly. When watching a college or pro game, it is easy for me to recognize players who have this quality. It truly separates them from others.

Again, I will go back to a great American player who grew up in Europe at a young age, Kobe Bryant. Kobe was taught to dribble and shoot properly. He understood without individual skill development he would never reach his potential. He did play high school in Philadelphia, but spent his time in the off-season training, not playing games.

Kobe had some "God gifts" that cannot be taught. He is 6'6," with the ideal basketball body. He was athletic with a big wing span, very similar to many American players that are playing in the NBA today. What separates Kobe from them was that he had been taught correctly. He was taught not only individual skills, but the mental approach needed to become the best he could be.

So many players today who have Kobe's physical attributes have the same potential to be great, but without being taught the foundation needed, will be labeled "good" and finish their careers with unrealized potential.

I often use the term "basketball dancing" when I initially begin working with kids. I relate this type of training to "dancing with the stars." Anyone can learn how to dance if they have a person training them who understands the basics of how to move efficiently, which is initiated by the feet.

After many years in my professional training business, I have the knowledge to improve anyone's balance. Most would be surprised at how fast the body learns how to move. A person can teach their body to do anything!

And it doesn't matter what level of player I am training. If they have never worked on using their weak foot, they all struggle. College and pro players are amazed when they can perform a drill so fluidly using their dominant foot and cannot do the drill when asked to use their weak foot.

The thing players do the most in a game is run. But basketball running is a lot of lateral movement and changes of direction. In other words, basketball running is confined to a small area with sudden turns. If players only use their coordinated foot, the majority of the time they are taking more steps than needed and turning the wrong way half of the time.

If their feet are equally balanced, they will be moving efficiently using the proper foot getting them from point A to point B. Efficiently means taking less steps. This translates into moving quickly from point A to point B.

The basic skills of shooting, ball handling and passing have always been the primary fundamentals learned to be a good basketball player. Today's game is played by players so much faster and more athletic. The real competitive edge comes from learning body balance as a part of every fundamental skill that is taught. The right drills will ensure that a player learns body balance at the same time that all the other fundamentals are being worked on. This enables a player to achieve real quickness when performing the primary fundamentals.

When I train elementary or middle school kids, high school, college or pros, I teach footwork and body balance at all times. That is where we start. Doing everything in basketball efficiently, using fewer steps, is the real competitive edge and provides players the chance to compete at the next level. At any level!

If you want to help your child really learn just how good they can be playing the game of basketball, the skill of body balance is as important as anything for their individual skill development and competitive edge. Find a skill development instructor in your area who understands how to teach this.

In an article written about Steph Curry, the 2015 and 2016 NBA MVP, he related his style of play to a ballet dancer. The reporter wrote the following comments made by two professional ballet dancers after watching Steph play:

> "What I see the most when I watch Steph is the incredible coordination he has with his arms, his legs and the way he handles the ball," Domitro, 29, said before drawing a comparison between their respective disciplines and referring to the way male dancers support women as they execute a lift or a jump. "We don't use a ball, you know. We use a woman. But the way he dribbles the ball is the way we handle a woman on stage. There's a certain sense of musicality to the way his body works," Lustig said. "It looks like he's moving in a slightly different dimension as everyone else, and I think that ties into his sheer speed and power and control – incredible, unbelievable control. And that's what you want in a dancer." [2]

What is extremely important to understand when reading about Steph's ability is that he was NOT born with this ability! Just like Kenny Anderson, his body size is not what separates him from others. When he was coming out of high school, big time college basketball programs actually questioned his size and lean body as their reasons not to recruit him.

His formula to become the best he could be also can be achieved by anyone. His shooting and dribbling skills were taught properly at an early age. He was taught how

---

2   Scott Cacciola, *New York Times*, November 24 2015, The Artistry of Stephen Curry

crucial was the connection his feet have to his upper body when creating moves. He also was taught to have the mindset to become the best he could be – which was all about his work ethic. This is something else to keep in mind. His off-seasons as a youth basketball player were not spent playing games. He never played in the Travel Team system.

Key to Remember:

- This chapter is all about the "make or break it" considerations a parent must take into account when deciding how their child can reach their potential. Your child can choose to stay the course many others are following in the US because parents have never heard anyone talk of other ways for them to improve. Hopefully, what I am sharing will help your child take the road less traveled and look further into how to get the real performance edge.
- No matter what sport is watched or played, initial movement of the body comes from the feet. This is key in the fundamental teaching of basketball. This is especially true with the small space the game is played on, having a player's body move in all different directions, along with going from being an offensive player to having to play defense in a split second.
- Understanding how a player's dominant leg/foot controls the majority of their movements should give them the knowledge to move more efficiently when playing the game. Not being able to use their weak foot will have them turning the wrong way, stopping quickly and taking a lot more steps than needed.
- Sometimes we overlook, or don't think about, how great players reached such levels. We often incorrectly think they were born with their gifts. There is only one common denominator shared among them which is available for anyone to use for their own success. They all were taught the proper techniques in the skills of dribbling and shooting. They have the ability to use either foot equally, and a great work ethic putting the majority of their time into individual training.

CHAPTER 9

Shooting .... A Lost Art

"If you want something new, you have to stop doing something old."
— PETER DRUCKER

The mechanics of the "jump shot" has become a lost art. The proper mechanics of shooting is one of the toughest skills to learn. If your child does not learn how to shoot the ball correctly, in theory, they are practicing a bad habit every time they shoot in practice or games.

Shooting is not being taught in America anymore, and it is very evident watching our players on the college level struggle to make jump shots.

In an article I read, "When Coaches Make No Sense," by *Pro Shot*, a Midwest scouting service asked over 1000 college and high school coaches a simple question. "Is shooting important?" The answer was a resounding, "Yes!" from 96% of college coaches, and 86% of high school coaches. [3] They were also asked, "How many more wins do you think you would get if your team were better shooters?" High school coaches believed they could achieve 6-8 more wins, and college coaches believed they would win 8-10 more games a season.

The coaches were then asked if they taught shooting during the season. Eight percent of high school and six percent of college coaches said, "Yes." I completely understand this statistic because during the season it is about a team getting ready for competition and winning the next game. But it is just one more example of why individual skill development and working on skills like shooting must be focused on in the off-season.

---

3 Pro Shot, *Pro Shot Shooting System*, August, 21, 2015

Another question asked was, "Do you feel knowledgeable about teaching shooting to your players?" Remarkably, only four percent of high school coaches and fourteen percent of college coaches said, "Yes."

The lack of skill teaching has been going on for years and it all traces back to kids who start out in the sport having no idea of the importance of being taught the proper technique when shooting. They truly believe if they just keep playing more, their shots will get better with time.

Coaches all agree shooting is important. They feel if their teams could shoot better, they would have more wins. But they really don't feel comfortable teaching shooting. If it is so important then why aren't more coaches taking the time to learn how to teach shooting? You cannot expect players to think it is that important if it is not a point of emphasis in the teaching process.

Trying to change a shot is difficult for several reasons, the biggest one being that until a player becomes comfortable with the correct technique, which takes time, they should not play competitively because they will revert back to what feels good. What feels good is a player's old shot. I have attempted to help many players with their shot, but very few had the discipline to stay away from their old habit. Playing games was more important to them.

Without having the right knowledge, parents assume their child's individual needs are being met. Parents need to ensure your children are focused on learning this skill as early in their development as possible. Find a resource who not only understands what needs to be taught, but is very good at its teaching.

The skill of shooting is a big edge for your child in making any team at any level of play. Trust me when I say if your child also wants to one-day play college basketball, this skill will be the deciding factor to getting on a college coach's radar and getting evaluated. Your child does not have to be a product of the environment where little or no instruction happens when it comes to shooting correctly. Your child can – and should – be taught the skill of shooting!

Teaching Proper Shooting Form Starts with The Lower Body

The little bit of shooting instruction I see happening at all is being done by volunteer coaches and parents. All the emphasis is focused on the shooting arm. I have watched and listened to all sorts of ways being taught about how the shot should be taken. The instruction and communication covers about ten percent of what is needed to shoot properly.

Without including the lower body into the learning process, becoming a good shooter is just not going to happen. Think about every time you see someone shoot. There is movement with the legs. That is crucial to becoming a shooter.

I always tell parents before I start to teach shooting that I will first concentrate on balance and squaring the body up. This has everything to do with legs and feet. The leg muscles are the brains behind the correct flow. Your leg muscles are responsible for the arc, squaring your body, soft touch and range, among others.

If I started teaching the shooting motion of the arm first, without lower body movement, the learning process would be very difficult. It would be putting the cart before the horse. This all goes back to believing in the training philosophy of how to become a quicker player. No matter what skill your child practices, they need to always emphasize feet and legwork.

Shot Quickness Comes from What Happens BEFORE You Catch the Ball

Quickness has to be attained in all phases of the game. Knowing how to shoot quickly is crucial for being able to play at high levels. I have evaluated so many players who had the reputation of being shooters. They had good form, but it took them so long to shoot after receiving the ball. They would never be able to get their shot off when playing against faster, bigger and stronger players.

How long does it take for a player to shoot after they receive the ball? This has become an essential statistic when evaluating a shooter. This is very similar to when football coaches are always focused on how fast a quarterback can get rid of the ball. They always talk about the quarterback's footwork being the key to a quick release. Basketball shooting is very much the same.

Shot quickness gives players the ability to take uncontested jump shots. An uncontested jump shot is taken without a defender's hand close to the ball or in a player's face just before it is released. The athleticism of today's players makes their defensive recovery time extremely fast.

Spotting up to take a quick jump shot begins before receiving the ball, preparing the feet to catch the ball so the player is able to go right into their shot as the ball is received. A player cannot be a quick shooter without this ability. If players wait to receive the ball to set their feet it will take too long and they may have the prettiest form, but will never get their shot off.

Catch and Shoot Vs Catch, Drop and Shoot

The final piece to being a quick shooter is the movement of the ball going into the shot. I use a phrase when teaching shot quickness. "Catch and shoot," not "catch, drop and shoot."

When I say "drop" I mean moving the ball down towards the player's waist before shooting. The ball is in the player's hands too long. It is very important to understand the final stage of the shot. The arm and wrist have nothing to do with shot quickness. It's all about preparing the feet to catch the ball. Catching the ball in the right position so the player can catch and shoot quickly is what gives them the motion and tempo required to get their shot off effectively.

I train kids as young as 3rd grade. My initial instructions on shooting begins with body balance and the position of the ball. This gives them the tools to automatically become quick shooters. Learning this skill properly will put your child on an enjoyable and rewarding basketball journey. There are roster spots on all levels for your child if they have learned to be a shooter.

You can use the perspective I have shared in this chapter to help you choose a resource in your community to teach your child to shoot. Search for the shooting skills trainer that believes in these same philosophies and methodologies.

Key to Remember

- Shooting without the proper mechanics means that every time your child shoots he or she is practicing the wrong way, and creating bad habits.
- In Chapter 8 I talked about how the lower body is crucial in learning how to play the entire game correctly. The upper body movement that happens when shooting gets all the attention, but to become a good shooter the shot has to start using the player's feet and legs.
- Don't assume the minimal instructions your child is getting about their shooting is sufficient, or that their shots will just get better over time by repetition alone. How your son or daughter is being taught how to shoot should be an area of concern. Teaching the proper technique is done with a great deal of knowledge, and it is a process which takes time.

CHAPTER 10

Ball Handling

"If you train hard, you'll not only be hard, you'll be hard to beat."
– HERSCHEL WALKER

all handling covers many aspects of the game, and the one we usually relate to and think of first is dribbling. Like shooting, it is overlooked by our youth coaches resulting in a domino effect. This skill is all about hand coordination. Catching and passing a ball is a major part of ball handling. The only way for a player to become good with their hands is through intense, individual dribbling drills, but many coaches today cannot fundamentally teach dribbling.

When done properly, the ball must hit the floor and return to the player's hand as quickly as possible. The ball is released from the hand by the fingertips. They are the most important part of the hand. Fingertip coordination and strength are critical to becoming a good basketball player. Your child's fingertips can only get better by first dribbling correctly.

The original way of teaching ball handling was done with individual stationary drills that dealt with coordinating both hands and fingertips, along with drills working on hand quickness. If a player had any desire to play youth basketball, getting this knowledge and practicing it was mandatory. These drills connected so many moving parts that are needed when playing. Today they are just an afterthought, if taught at all. Dribbling is taught today with the emphasis on moving, skipping the initial instructions on how to dribble correctly.

Fingers versus Palm of Hand

In the mid-nineties, as more game play was growing and being emphasized more so than individual skill development, fundamental instruction emphasis on dribbling properly ended. Dribbling with one hand on the side of the ball became prevalent as players watched NBA greats like Allen Iverson make swooping moves. This became the fundamental way U.S. players dribbled. This totally takes the fingertips out of being used because the palm controls the action.

As this concept took over, officials on the collegiate level were caught between a rock and a hard place. Everyone was breaking the "palming" rule. Officials began blowing their whistles at an alarmingly high rate.

The officials finally started to adjust the "palming" rule. Decisions like this have handicapped the American youth players' ability to move quickly when dribbling because the longer the ball is "not" in a player's hand, the slower they become. Only in the United States are you permitted to break the original palming rule. Everywhere else it is a violation.

This is another skill that is very seldom taught. When it is being taught, the initial dribble movement is to roll the hand from the side of the ball. This is another example how today's instructors are themselves products of never being taught properly how to dribble. To be an effective dribbler the hand has to be on top of the ball. This enables a player to get the ball to the floor as quickly as possible in order for it to return to him quickly.

The sweeping palm to palm dribbling of Allen Iverson was done as an "offensive move" that very few are capable of performing, but in American youth basketball today this has become the most important move for kids to learn when starting out in elementary school.

I never realized I would be spending so much of my training sessions emphasizing the right way to dribble. This is because, for the most part, it has not been a focus as an important fundamental skill.

I have two dribbling rules at all times in my training sessions. The player must pound the ball to the floor with his hand on top. If the player doesn't pound the ball, they must do two pushups for soft dribbling. If the player dribbles with their hand on the side of the ball, they must do three pushups.

Being able to dribble properly enhances a player's game in so many ways. Teaching their hand to be situated properly on the top of the ball takes practice. When a player repeatedly is able to follow through with their fingertips pounding the ball to the floor, it adds strength to the wrist. This helps to coordinate fingertips, which adds to the overall ball handling skill set.

The biggest impact incorrect dribbling has had on the game is that players today aren't able to coordinate their fingertips. Yes, a player can coordinate their fingertips.

This is essential to being able to consistently control accuracy when passing, shooting and being able to dribble the ball hard to the floor. Fingers are the last to touch the ball when performing these movements.

Fingertip control is essential to becoming a good shooter. Also, if taught properly, the ball partially rests on a player's fingers when setting up to take a shot, which means to be a good shooter, dribbler or passer, the fingertips play a big role.

In my career I had the opportunity to personally watch two of the greatest ball-handlers ever to play. I was introduced to how important dribbling drills were to ball-handling by Pete Mavarich. He explained and demonstrated how fingertips are vital to dribbling correctly, passing with accuracy and shooting with a precision. He talked about his finger pads being the catalyst behind his creativity.

Observing Kenny Anderson's ball-handling skills for two years during practice and in games was another experience watching an incredible dribbler. He performed ball-handling skills that were done in a blink of an eye. Kenny would make passes off the dribble with such precision it would amaze anyone who witnessed it. I would often find myself saying, "Did he just do what I think he did?" so many times after performing an incredible quick dribbling move. Afterwards I would ask Kenny to show me what he did.

I cannot emphasize enough how imperative it is that working endlessly on proper dribbling drills will take your child's talent to unbelievable levels.

Command The Ball. Don't Allow It to Dictate to You.

Practicing dribbling, body balance and foot coordination at the same time are essential to becoming a high-level dribbler. Powerful dribbling can help a player succeed in many ways, including the ability to pass immediately, shoot off the dribble and using the body when driving the lane.

I constantly preach, "the ball should never dictate how you move." When dribbling, the player commands the ball, so he or she is able to move or pass in a split second.

Too many players miss out on offensive opportunities today because their feet are not set when they receive the ball. Combine that with bad dribbling habits, and opportunities are lost to being offensively effective.

I rarely see a player anymore who dribbles correctly. When I do that player immediately becomes a great example for others, showing how they are always ready to move into their shot or make a pass. The need to correct bad dribbling habits almost always falls on deaf ears because our basketball community truly believes they have learned the game correctly.

Young players cannot be faulted for the way they think. They are just trying to emulate the older players above them. When the majority of American college players dribble, their initial move places their hand on the side of the ball. Why wouldn't our youth see this as the correct way to dribble?

It is always rewarding when a player buys into and understands what I am teaching even though it is not something common as part of today's game. There was a young kid who I started training in the 7th grade, and we worked diligently through high school. All of the emphasis was on body coordination, dribbling and shooting skills. It became obvious to me after his sophomore year that he had college potential. It was all up to him how hard he wanted to work, so we did not know the college level he could compete at. He never let up going into his senior year and wound up being recruited heavily by Division I schools. This was a kid who, without the body coordination and learning the proper technique in dribbling and shooting, would have been a typical American youth player who had potential, but did not know how to use it.

His name was Chase Anderson. He received a scholarship to play at the Air Force Academy. During the recruiting process coaches would comment not just on his shooting, but about how he was so under control with the ball when dribbling and passing. Chase and I knew it all came from his body being so coordinated. Chase has told me,

> "I know for a fact the Division I offers I received were a direct result of dribbling harder and training my legs and feet to move stronger. I was simply a more efficient mover on the court than most of my peers."

Coordinate Your Feet and Hands

It is crucial for your child to have good footwork when dribbling if they hope to ever be an effective offensive player. A player's feet dictate where they are going. Having their feet and hands equally coordinated when dribbling makes them very difficult to guard.

San Antonio Spurs guard, Tony Parker, has a very unique dribbling technique. It is explosive and quick. No matter what hand he is dribbling with, left or right, he uses the same foot to push off of to explode to the basket. If he is dribbling off a screen going to his right, he uses his right hand to dribble. When he sees an opening, he pushes with his right foot to attack the basket.

This is abnormal because the natural movement when dribbling with a player's right hand is to use the left foot as the lead, but Tony Parker uses his feet in the quickest way.

Passing

Ball-handling skills go beyond dribbling. Passing and catching are critical in becoming a good player. To achieve quickness when passing, a player must make hard, fast passes by following through with the fingertips. Throwing soft passes makes it easy for defenders to steal the ball, or enables them to defend multiple players at the same time.

I like to use the expression "hide the ball." This requires a player to use their body to protect the ball when passing. In a half court setting, the opportunity to pass the ball with two hands very seldom presents itself because defenders play the ball hard with aggressive hands. Learning how to pass protecting the ball starts with the player's feet and toes.

For a player to pass successfully, they must pivot, using their toes as the axis to move free of the defender. This gives the player the ability to move quickly in all directions. Pivoting plays a big part in all aspects of the game. Performing pivots quickly requires the use of the toes immediately upon stopping to pass.

To become an effective passer, the player first has to coordinate their hands and legs equally. Learning to use the weak side of their body comes from other skill sets. Dribbling drills, both stationary and moving, along with off the move shooting drills, will give the player the tools to become a quick passer.

A player becomes one dimensional if they cannot use both sides of their body equally when passing. They then use only one side of the court to make good passes and become vulnerable to having passing turnovers.

When it comes to actually making the pass, your child's lower body is used to execute this movement, making it strong and well balanced. The force behind any good pass comes from the legs, which is why a player must have body coordination. Using the upper body as the main catalyst behind the pass is a turnover ready to happen. Without quick foot speed and lower body strength players can never become effective passers.

As an example, let's just say your child has not worked on toe pivoting and has not coordinated their weak foot. If double-teamed and by necessity their pivot foot is their uncoordinated one, not only will they not be able to use their toes to move their body, the double team is going to make them look bad, possibly forcing a turnover. The reverse side of that is also true: if your child was comfortable working with the uncoordinated foot, they would be able to successfully get out of that type of predicament.

I have briefly explained the basic instructions one needs to perform offensive skills correctly and they all connected to each other. As an example, players cannot be good shooters without fingertip control, and to attain that they have to dribble correctly. All of this ties into body coordination.

The best thing you can do is find a skills instructor who understands not only how to teach all the different fundamentals, but also how they are all dependent upon one another. Teaching with the right creative drills is critical to ensuring your child instinctively puts it all together.

Key to Remember

- Dribbling is the most important of all basketball skills. It is linked to shooting, passing and catching because, when performed correctly, a player is developing their hands and fingertips.
- Similar to shooting becoming an afterthought in how the game is being taught in this country, dribbling incorrectly has gone on for so long that coaches on the youth, high school and college level have accepted it. There is very little concern for how it should be done. The younger coaches who have come through the era of playing many off-season games rather than focusing on individual skill development don't understand the importance of the connection fingertips have with so many other phases of the game.
- Dribbling properly is not a long learning process, but doing it correctly immediately puts your child on a path to improve in many skill development areas quickly.
- Understanding the connection between dribbling and foot coordination is crucial if a player wants to move quickly and efficiently. Not being able to use both feet equally will have a negative impact on how productive your child can be when dribbling.
- Passes are all dictated by the lower body being able to use both feet equally. It is very important for being able to pass effectively in any direction.

- Having good ball handling skills through dribbling drills gives players the ability to pass with either hand and use their fingertips to follow through, making the passes forceful and accurate.
- It is so important to see the connection each skill has with one another because they are all needed to be successful when performing them.

CHAPTER 11

Defense

*"Only those who risk going too far can possibly
find out how far one can go."*
– T.S. ELIOT

Offensive skills might not be good enough to make a team. They may not be good enough to earn a player more playing time if they are on a team. Having the mindset to play defense is strongly taken into consideration when coaches are making decisions for which players will make the team and earn more playing time.

Half of a game is played on the defensive end but in the minds of most parents and players, it is not part of an evaluation by coaches. Coaches on all levels will evaluate both offensive skills and defensive skills. Players should never disregard a focus on improving their defensive capabilities.

As a college coach in preparation to play an opponent, the majority of our time was on the defensive side of the ball. Players were given assignments based on their defensive skills. Listening to parents and players in high school or college complain about the lack of playing time, they typically argued their case by describing their offensive skills against those getting more playing time. They rarely even mention the defensive side of the ball which weighs so heavily on playing time in a coach's mind.

Again, the over-emphasis on playing games rather than learning how to play has negatively impacted our youth basketball system. To add to the problem, playing two to four games in a day has made teaching good defense nearly impossible.

It is a challenge to defend a talented offensive player. This can only be accomplished by having the desire to do it, along with lower body coordination. This means being able to push off both feet equally and using upper leg strength to stay low enough to move aggressively.

Defense is basketball running, which is extremely stressful to your legs. To expect someone to play good defense when playing more than one game a day is absurd. Having tired legs is the root cause behind many things a player ends up not doing well in a game.

Typically, tired legs start to have a negative impact when a player is on the defensive side of the floor. He will tend to let up and rest at that time because he doesn't worry about being on defense and defending against a player making a sharp move against him.

The number of games played in the off-season, weekly tournaments and multiple game days, has made losing too acceptable. This happens for a lot of reasons, but the main cause is that there is very little time to digest a win or loss. There is no time to play the game over and over in your mind, dissecting the good and bad. It is all about quickly putting the past game behind you because you have to move quickly onto the next.

In theory, defense is a part of the game that should have different strategies with every opponent. The majority of the time, not knowing the opponent takes strategies out of the game plan, so defense cannot be stressed with any level of real importance.

In my years at Suwanee Sports Academy, we sponsored many tournaments where we had college officials calling the games. They would tell me Travel Ball games were the hardest basketball games to officiate because of the lack of defensive containment on the ball. So many possessions turn into five men against four.

The teams have no philosophy or structure, so players are constantly out of position along with being tired. This leads to reaching instead of moving their feet, and all of these situations lead to fouls. Calling a lot of fouls creates a hostile spectator environment because they believe the officials are at fault. But the truth is bad defense is creating the problem. No one is to blame about the Travel Team system defense because to teach good defensive play takes time, with a lot of practices.

Rebounding

Defensive rebounding is the final thing to do as a good defender. The non-athletic basketball player needs this skill to overcompensate for his lack of jumping ability.

Since playing games in the off-season has become such an emphasis for youth basketball in the United States, this individual skill of being a good rebounder has diminished. Molding players into rebounders cannot be done by just screaming out the term during game situations or telling them during time outs that is what they need to do. This skill has to be practiced over and over. It has to be done instinctively. First, it has to be a habit going to the basket. Then, the technique of boxing out has to be taught to give a better opportunity to get the ball.

Boxing out has not been taught for a long time. While coaching high school basketball for a three-year period starting in 2011, I emphasized boxing out in practice every day. I was pleased as my players started to transfer their newly learned rebounding skills to the games.

Officials were constantly calling my guys for fouling. They kept telling my players they "could not do that." It was sad to watch. Good rebounding techniques were being viewed as fouls. It showed how much of the game is not being taught anymore. Referees were seeing techniques used that were not common to them, so in their view they thought they must be fouls.

How Coaches Evaluate Ability to Play Defense

College coaches view a player's ability to play defense by evaluating how quickly he or she can get from point A to point B while in a defensive stance.

1. On The Ball. This defense is all about lateral movement. Is a player capable of containing his man when he is dribbling? Containing means keeping him in front of you. Getting beat on the ball creates 5 against 4 situations. This is where the percentages work against a team. If players struggle to contain the ball it will eventually affect playing time.
2. Help and Recovery. This is off the ball defense, helping a teammate defend his man, but having the ability to get back (recover) and continue defending your man when he receives the ball.
3. Transition Defense. Is a player observant enough to get back on defense after an offensive possession to stop fast breaks? Then find his man and get into position to defend his man.

The most unique player I ever recruited was Karl Brown from Chipola Junior College. He was a 6'1" point guard from Leister, England, who got my attention watching him play defense. Karl was a good ball-handler. He lacked a jump shot but made up for it on the defensive end as a relentless on-the-ball defender. Karl had a major impact on our success the year we made it to the Final Four coming off the bench. He went on to play pro ball in England, and now coaches back in his hometown of Leister.

To this day the most rewarding story I have heard concerning my training methods occurred after my first year as a player development instructor. After leaving college coaching, I had, for the first time, put together a training philosophy and training program that incorporated the skills of footwork, shooting and ball-handling. These were individual training sessions even though I taught in small groups of up to 8 participants at one time. They lasted an hour. In that time, I touched on all the skills. Footwork was the most important. Instead of taking time to do just footwork only, I integrated it to ensure an emphasis while doing shooting or ball-handling drills.

The only worry I had about my training sessions initially was that I was not including defense skill development in my curriculum. I only had an hour so I had to pick and choose what I felt would develop their skills quicker.

As I was preparing to begin my second season of skill development sessions, I conducted an "open house" question and answer session for parents. The first comment I heard was from a parent who had a boy and a girl playing in high school. Their coaches had mentioned that their defense had really improved.

I immediately knew why. Even though we never did a defensive drill, we had such an emphasis on footwork and using both feet equally along with turning the correct way. This meant increasing the ability to take less steps when moving from Point A to Point B.

Key to Remember

- Parents and players need to take defense as seriously as offense because half of the game is played on defense. Coaches take playing defense very seriously.
- When comparing your child to others, if they are lacking offensive skills, they can balance that by putting their attention on being a good defender. Because most kids don't pay attention to being a good defender, a player who is willing to learn how to be a good defender stands out among others.
- Coaches make decisions on a player's playing time at the higher the level of play, usually starting in high school, based on their defensive capabilities.
- Rebounding is a player's final responsibility when playing defense. It is a skill that needs to be taught. Simply yelling "rebound" is not going to accomplish this task. The first objective is to consistently go to the basket on a shot. Next is to box out a player which is performing a back pivot initiated by the feet.

These two things have to become a habit which can only be accomplished by repetitions when practicing.

- Spectators tend to rate a player's defensive skills on how they cover the ball because that is what they are following while watching the game. But better defenders are off the ball in a good position to help out if needed.

CHAPTER 12

The Right Mindset - Building Your Game to UNLOCK Your Potential

*"Commitment separates those who live their dreams
from those who live their lives regretting the
opportunities they have squandered."*
– BILL RUSSELL

The right mindset and character must be built to really pursue and build your child's game with any hope of becoming a good player. I do not think I am going out on the limb when saying players must become obsessed to succeed. It takes obsession and commitment to create an "everyday discipline." Ninety percent of a player's training comes from within. This is a completely different approach than how youth basketball operates today. But this approach must have structure. A player's desire to become the best they can become in hopes of playing college basketball is going to take tremendous discipline and dedication.

The off-season needs to be devoted to improving all aspects of the game to learn how to coordinate a player's body to shoot and dribble properly. The biggest obstacle will be creating this mindset that is so foreign to how your child's friends are approaching the game. This process will not only improve your child's basketball skills, but will also build tremendous character traits that can be used by your son or daughter throughout their lives.

Here are some tips to get started:

Attitude - Players must attack their training with the same effort and competitiveness as they do with games. It cannot be turned on and off like a faucet. If it is only a matter of going through the motions in training, it will transfer over to the game. That is a recipe for disaster. Remember: if the work is put in, the results will come."

> "You have to have the work ethic, you have to
> push yourself and not be satisfied."
> – KOBE BRYANT

Intensity - Go hard every time. This is the most important thing to remember. Many have heard the saying, "Practice at game speed" or, "Game shots at game speed." Players train to play the game. They are working toward improving their skills in games. The best way to do that is to go harder in practice and push themselves to the limits to develop their skills faster. This will make the game easier. Don't go through the motions, because fatigue leads to bad habits.

> "Perfection is not attainable. But if we chase
> perfection, we can catch excellence."
> – VINCE LOMBARDI

Concentration - Players need to be focused if they want their skills to develop. Get in a zone. Your mind tells your muscles what to do, so concentrating at the highest level is critical. Learned concentration creates instinctive action.

> "What do I mean by concentration? I mean focusing
> totally on the business at hand and commanding your
> body to do exactly what you want it to do."
> – ARNOLD PALMER

Repetition - This cannot be avoided in workouts. Combine the right drills and exercises with a high quantity of quality reps. This is the key to a player reaching their full potential. Players need to turn fundamentals into a habit, and that is done by passionate repetition

> "Repetition of the same thought or physical
> action develops into a habit which,
> repeated frequently enough, becomes an automatic reflex."
> – Norman Vincent Peale

Competing Against Yourself - To achieve discipline in developing a competent off-season daily routine, goals need to be set. This will keep up motivation and drive to constantly improve.

> "My God-given talent is my ability to stick with
> training longer than anybody else."
> – Herschel Walker

Practicing on Your Own

Train to play the game, don't play to train. Stay focused on the big picture, which is to become the best a player can be. This is a process that can only be accomplished by spending long hours with individual training.

It is easy to start something. The challenge comes from staying consistent. There will be days where a player won't feel like working out or working hard. What they do on these days will define their off-season. There is nothing wrong with a player taking a break to let their body rest. But a player can't allow themselves to skip a day simply because they don't feel like working. Your child must be challenged to be the best every day. The key is to organize their training sessions with weekly and daily practice plans.

Scheduling – Your child needs to set up a weekly calendar, penciling in all of the planned activities so scheduled times can be planned to workout.

Location - Pick a location that is accessible. It does not have to be an extravagant area, just spacious enough to run and dribble. A backyard is an ideal location. It is more comfortable and private.

Preparation - Preparing to train is just as important as the training itself. Without this critical first step, going to the gym will be a haphazard plan. I cannot emphasize how important it is to maximize the time by training "efficiently," including:

1.   Knowing how to dribble and shoot correctly.
2.   Maximizing time and effort.
3.   Establishing goals for every drill so that a specific level of performance can be achieved.
4.   Keeping it all manageable. Don't start out with goals that feel overwhelming.
5.   Chart daily results. Regularly evaluate and assess the effectiveness of goals.

Having the right mindset will put your son or daughter in a unique category.

Key to Remember

▪   To accomplish your child's basketball goals, it is critical they have structure physically and mentally on how this process will work, planning weekly and daily workout plans just as a coach would do to prepare for a team practice. This is the most important part of your child's journey. You can have all the knowledge on what is needed to do, but without execution, they will not succeed. Establishing a solid work ethic is easy to say but extremely hard to do. But once your child gets going, it will become part of their character.

▪   The discipline part of your child working on their own will be difficult because this is not what their friends or our basketball community believes is important.

▪   It is very important to understand how your child should practice on their own without a coach or trainer pushing them. Just going through the motions will be a waste of time, and will produce very little improvement.

▪   Productive, individual training comes from putting some type of goal to the drills. This can either be setting a time limit, or putting a specific number to the drill before it is complete. Just putting the time in is not the objective. It is the quality of the time spent training that is needed for continued improvement.

▪   I talked about the formula that is needed to become the best a player can be. Knowing how to dribble and shoot correctly, along with individual player development and work ethic is key. The critical part of that formula is knowing how to practice shooting and dribbling properly to avoid practicing bad habits.

- You and your child need to regularly get input from reliable basketball people who can critique strengths and weaknesses and thus plan positive workouts.

Be sure to access bonus content as my gift to you

www.KevinCantwellBasketball.com/p/gifts

SECTION 4

Understand The Exposure and Evaluation Process

"Any fool can know. Point is to understand."
– ALBERT EINSTEIN

My intent with this section of the book is to educate basketball parents with kids of all ages about what it takes to get the attention of a college coach to get evaluated. This part of the book is not just for parents of high school kids. It is never too early to build a solid foundation of knowledge about how college coaches evaluate and recruit players. This is one of the most misunderstood topics of such high interest to so many parents, players and all stakeholders within the grassroots basketball community in the US.

A good evaluation leads to being recruited. I will talk about the myths and misconceptions relating to how college coaches locate players to evaluate. I will also share insights on how you can take charge of getting in front of college coaches instead of waiting and expecting them to find you.

My college recruiting and coaching experience is with men but my familiarity with women started to evolve during my time with Suwanee Sports Academy when we hosted boys and girl's events that attracted college coaches. There are very few disparities between the women's and men's recruiting topics.

Things have changed a great deal in youth basketball in America over the years. Understanding how things work now and the history regarding how they used to work is very important when making the right decisions for and with your child. All parents in our youth basketball culture need to understand this current system has not been around forever and why it is so popular.

It is important to know getting a college coach to evaluate your son or daughter is a big accomplishment. It doesn't just happen. You need to do the right things at the right time to make it happen. This section will provide you all the guidance you need.

CHAPTER 13

Understanding the Odds of Playing College Basketball

"If we did all the things we were capable of doing,
we would literally astound ourselves."

– THOMAS EDISON

n this chapter I will give you the knowledge to be able to determine the roster spots your son or daughter is qualified for at the college level so realistic goals can be set and a plan of action created to accomplish.

Open roster spots in middle and high school are usually common knowledge because of the accessible information throughout the local community. When it comes time to access information about college rosters to set realistic goals for playing college ball, typically most parents and players don't know how to get started.

It continues to astonish me every year how unrealistic high school players are when it comes to their abilities to play college ball. When they do have the ability to play in college they are not practical about their right level. This type of thinking keeps kids from playing in college because they don't have the in-depth knowledge needed to make the right decisions.

To set attainable goals for playing college basketball, parents and players need a realistic view of their chances. They need an approach to identify the college roster spots available they are a fit for, then consider the competition for those spots.

As parents, we all have a tendency to be biased when it comes to our kids. It is critical you are realistic when considering the right college level for your child's ability to compete. His or her goals will be unattainable if they are not realistic.

I will give you ways to determine what college levels of play you should be investigating. The ideal time to start this process is right after high school freshman year, but can be done anytime during your child's high school years.

There are approximately 4,000 college basketball roster spots available each year. The numbers and odds are challenging when compared to the total number of players eligible to play college basketball. This is why it is important for a player to improve their odds by understanding the process every college coach goes through when identifying recruiting targets.

Not understanding the ins and outs of this process really lowers a player's chances. The key is not to let the numbers bring you down. It is about having the right approach, plan, skills and relationships. Going about things the right way will enable you to work the right plan. And like any plan, you have to manage and navigate through the obstacles. Only then will your chances of success increase.

Remember today's college coaches work within an imperfect process. They try to make the best decisions they can, but even then the system is not perfect and mistakes can be made.

If you know what to do and when to do it, you can guide and influence the way decisions are made and improve your child's odds of playing college basketball. It is important to know what you are up against, and build your plan accordingly.

Available Roster Spots

The minimal number of roster spots coaches can recruit each year is a critical part of their recruiting strategy, and is foremost in their minds. This is demonstrated on the recruiting trail. As coaches are constantly asking other coaches, "How many players are you looking for?" or, "How many players can you bring in?" The answers for the most part will range from one to five players.

College basketball consists of five levels without considering junior colleges. This graph gives the number of basketball programs on each level and the number of roster spots that are available annually. I calculated an average of three recruits for each program.

	Men's Basketball		Women's Basketball	
NCAA Division I	351 Schools	1,053 Spots	349 Schools	1047 Spots
NCAA Division II	308 Schools	924 Spots	307 Schools	921 Spots
NCAA Division III	421 Schools	1,263 Spots	442 Schools	1326 Spots
NAIA Division I	105 Schools	315 Spots	105 Schools	315 Spots
NAIA Division II	125 Schools	375 Spots	124 Schools	372 Spots

So, we're looking at approximately 3930 total spots for men and 3981 for women. It is impossible to certify the exact number of open roster spots each year, but this is a close estimate. This number alone compared to the eligible players competing for these spots is a real eye opener.

In addition, all of these open spots have to be broken down by position. This makes it even more of a challenge getting evaluated. The advantage in recruiting always goes to the taller player because "you can't coach height," meaning a coach cannot teach you how to become taller.

Players Eligible for Recruitment

Coaches identify prospects from five different sources. There are approximately 160,000 high school seniors, 1500 post-graduate (prep schools), 6000 junior college players and an unlimited number of international players. College transfers also have an impact on available roster spots.

College coaches face so much pressure to win right away. This requires they focus on recruiting the more physically mature player. They then concentrate heavily on Prep School, Junior College and transfer players.

Post Graduate (Prep School)

There are approximately 1500 Postgraduate Prep players who have already graduated from high school. The potential of a college coach finding a prospect is very high within this type of player. The main reason is the majority of kids who attend these schools have college basketball potential. The deciding factor for players to attend these schools is that chances are good they will be exposed to and evaluated by college coaches.

There are three primary reasons why players choose the prep school path:

1. Physical maturity. Possibly the player was younger than most seniors in high school. This puts the player's physical maturity behind. An extra year to mature physically will put the player in a better position to make an impression on the college coach.
2. To improve as a player. A player may have been recruited in high school but not been satisfied with the schools showing interest. Their thinking is another year of playing might get the interest of different and higher level college basketball programs.
3. Academics. A player may not have qualified for college entrance test scores. Not having gotten an acceptable SAT/ACT score, players will graduate high school and take extra time trying to pass the college entrance exam by going to prep school.

A perfect example was a player I had been training. He played the point guard position. He had a good feel for the game. He was an excellent ball handler and could hit the open jump shot. I knew going into his senior year he had college talent but the challenge was convincing college coaches because he hadn't physically matured yet.

As the year progressed, I realized attending a postgraduate program was in his best interest. His decision to go in this direction proved to be correct. He chose a school where college coaches frequently watched practices and attended games. Before the season began he was already being recruited by low D1 schools. This was all he wanted.

One coach from a high major school offered him a guaranteed walk on spot. He chose the walk-on position because the coach was Rick Pinto at Louisville. He graduated from the University of Louisville, and had a great experience being part of a basketball program that went on to the Final Four in his junior season.

Junior College Players

There are approximately 6000 talented, eligible players every year at the junior college level that college coaches can choose from to evaluate. Coaches are attracted to junior college players because of their talent and physical maturity. Instead of signing an eighteen-year-old, a coach is getting a player two to three years older which is a big factor. We had great success at Georgia Tech recruiting junior college players and our reasoning was always based on needing experience right away.

International Players (Unlimited)

The game has gone global thanks to technology. Ease of communicating with players overseas has increased drastically. The immense growth is attributed to American basketball not producing skilled players. It is very common today to see more than two international players on a college roster. If we continue on the path of not developing fundamentally sound players in America, the number of international players playing college ball here will continue to grow.

Evaluating international players can be done in person or on video. The majority of college coaches do not travel out of the country because of the cost, but most programs on all levels are exploring this resource.

This process is not as difficult as it may seem. Usually there are entities who have control of the players in their prospective countries. For instance, when I was recruiting, I knew the contact person for players in Nigeria and Serbia. These representatives are now sending players over to play in high schools. This has helped the overseas player create another stepping-stone into the collegiate ranks.

It is very common to see a college roster with two or more players from the same country. This occurs because if a player is successful and has a good experience at a college, it opens the door for more players from the same country to be recruited.

College Transfers

Players transferring from one college basketball program to another is at an all-time high in men's basketball. In Division I alone, forty percent of players transfer after 2 years. In 2013, 455 players transferred. There were 604 transfers in 2014 and 700 in 2015.

Reasons for transfers vary from a coaching change, a player seeking more playing time or family situations. The negative impact is the decreasing number of roster spots for new players because for the most part transfers have to sit out a year. This reserves roster spots for five years for transferred players.

Understanding the numbers when it comes to the odds is very important, but let's not lose hope or sight of one very important thing. The odds can be beat if parents do the right things at the right time during their child's basketball journey.

Key to Remember

- Set realistic goals. Parents need to know their child's opportunities for roster spots and positions available along with who he or she is competing against. Making the team is always challenging. Occupying a college roster spot is difficult, but not impossible.
- There are approximately 4000 available roster spots yearly each for Men and Women's Basketball. They are spread amongst five levels of colleges--NCAA Division I, II, III and NAIA I and II.
- The coaches have four sources to recruit players: high school seniors, prep school players, junior college and international players. Being able to take the largest of these four sources, high school seniors, and shift their focus into the off-season and NCAA certified events has had a big, positive impact for college coaches.
- The international player is taking roster spots away from American kids. This will continue because the style they play is the missing piece college coaches cannot find in American kids.

CHAPTER 14

NCAA Takes Control of Travel Team Events

"The secret of change is to focus all your energy not on fighting the old but on building the new."
— SOCRATES

Effects Majority of High School Players

The rapid ascension of Travel Ball caught the attention of the National Collegiate Athletic Association (NCAA). Before then, the NCAA never really had a reason to distinguish high school play from outside competition. The NCAA guidelines, for the most part, pertained to what coaches could do during the academic year.

Coaches were traveling in new recruiting circles and the NCAA was struggling to get its hands around what was happening. Thus began the yearly NCAA rule changes for coaches involved in Travel Team competitions.

In the mid-1990s, coaches had approximately ninety-one days to evaluate tournaments. There were no restrictions on what events to attend. There were hundreds of Travel Team tournaments available for coaches to attend in the fall, spring and summer. Today college coaches have *eighteen days* to observe Travel Team Events.

In Chapter 2, I introduced a Travel Team culture that was different from the financial and competitive model on which the Travel Ball concept was founded. The original concept pitted sponsored teams against each other. The best against the best. Since the majority of the tournaments in the 90's were run by spinoff organizers, a new type of team was established. To make a distinction between the two systems, I will categorize them as "sponsored" and "non-sponsored" teams.

Sponsored Team

Sponsors support these teams. This gives team representatives or coaches the ability to recruit the best players in their state or region using the resources given to them by sponsors. A player's sponsorship package includes complimentary apparel, sneakers and team travel, which includes airline tickets, ground transportation (such as buses and vans), hotels and meal allowances. In other words, a full scholarship.

I recently read where an NBA player who went directly to the pros out of high school said he "has been a pro since he was 9 years old." He was on one of these sponsored teams and never had to pay for anything.

Some examples of sponsorship include:

1. Sports-related companies using their involvement in youth sports to help sell more of their products and services. Examples are Nike, Adidas and Reebok.
2. Former and present NBA players who went through the Travel Team system and want to financially assist players who cannot afford the cost to be on these teams. Examples are LeBron James (King James Shooting Stars), Chris Paul (CP3 All Stars) and Dwight Howard (D 12 Warriors).
3. Music companies with representatives who want to associate with the up and coming players. These representatives view this as an opportunity to assist players who cannot afford the cost. At the same time, they can create an impactful marketing vehicle if one of these players becomes successful in college or on the professional level.
4. Wealthy private citizens who love the game of basketball and care for the kids.

One hundred percent of the teams were sponsored in the beginning. The sponsors were Nike and Adidas. Now there are additional sources for sponsorships. Today, only about ten percent of Travel Teams are sponsored.

The winter months are crucial to sponsored team coaches because it is their recruiting window to evaluate and recruit prospects. To help fulfill team needs, coaches recruit by position, seeking point guards, perimeter players and bigs (forwards and centers).

This highly competitive process is defined by intense recruiting battles. Each sponsor team coach works to land the best players available each year. Without rules, this process turns into an "anything goes" environment. At times it gets into a bidding war offering more incentives to get players.

How competitive is it? For example, one state might have twenty 17U sponsored teams. The twenty sponsored team coaches are recruiting each winter to fill their rosters which average 15 spots. This provides college coaches a list of approximately 350 players to evaluate in that state.

Non-Sponsored Teams

The growth in numbers of these non-sponsored teams is the catalyst behind the financial success for tournament organizers. These team rosters consist of players from a small geographical area who may have played together for years. Parents, relatives or friends typically coach the team. The families, for the most part, pay for the team's expenses.

Because of their small recruiting bases, non-sponsored rosters have a difficult time recruiting players by position. It is not unusual to see a team with two or three players playing out of position.

NCAA Rules Impact Non-Sponsored Teams

As the Travel Team world grew in teams and tournaments, knowing it could not directly control their aspirations, the NCAA began to put limitations on how college coaches used the system to recruit.

While there have been many NCAA rule changes pertaining to Travel Teams over the years, there were two changes directly impacting grassroots participants:

1. NCAA Certification for All Events.
    To control events, the NCAA required the organizers to follow certain guidelines to become certified. Coaches are only allowed to attend certified events. The procedure to get an event certified is extensive.

    During the event the NCAA will have a representative monitoring the event, making sure the guidelines are followed. The interesting part is that no one really knew who the NCAA rep was. After the event all the participant contact information was required to be sent to the NCAA.
2. Limiting Days Coaches Can Attend NCAA Certified Events.
    There were many reasons why the NCAA slowly and gradually limited recruiting days coaches could attend tournaments. The most significant one was because these events were scheduled every weekend in the fall and spring. The majority of Division I programs could not utilize these opportunities because of expenses. This was giving the larger programs a huge advantage. To

bring it back into a better balance for all schools, the NCAA began to control the dates coaches could evaluate.

The time coaches could attend certified events had gone from 91 days in the 90's to eighteen days in 2014-2015. Six days are during two weekends in the spring, and twelve days are in July.

In the 90's when the non-sponsored team was established, there was about a five-year period where organizers did not give a great deal of attention to how they scheduled opponents. The schedules did not separate sponsored teams from others so it was very common that evaluators were watching games that were not very competitive. This was a period of time driving the myth that playing Travel Ball was the way for a college coach to see you play.

As the NCAA gradually eliminated recruiting days over a period of time, the tournament organizer worried. The financial stability of their businesses was being threatened. They had to eliminate tournaments because team registrations were dropping drastically without the college coaches attending.

Tournament organizers realized to put on a great event the schedule must have the sponsored teams playing each other. The best against the best. This would satisfy the evaluation needs of college coaches. To make up for the loss of tournaments the organizers began having mega-events to increase participant registrations.

Organizers of an NCAA certified tournament today want to have as many sponsored teams as possible to attract college coaches. This lures the non-sponsored teams to participate, believing the coaches are there to see everyone. A typical example of registered teams in a 1000 team tournament is 200 sponsored, 800 non-sponsored teams. Parents are not realizing that the coaches are there to see the 200 teams only.

Keys to Remember

- Sponsored team rosters are considered to have the best players in their state. Each player has been recruited to play their true position. Sponsored Teams make up only about 10% of all Travel Teams.
- Non-sponsored teams are made up of local players. There are frequently situations where players have to play out of position because of the makeup of the team.

- The drastic change for coaches has been the time restraints to locate possible prospects in high school. The number of days they have to evaluate at NCAA certified events is changing all the time. In order to follow the NCAA rules for the number of days college coaches can evaluate and recruit, their primary focus has become the players on sponsored teams only.

CHAPTER 15

How College Coaches Recruit Players – The Process

"There is nothing quite so useless as doing with great efficiency something that should not be done at all."
– PETER DRUCKER

College recruiting strategies are all dictated by the ever-changing guidelines imposed by the NCAA. Every high school athlete who wants to be evaluated must understand how the NCAA evaluation periods are used, and the rules coaches must abide by. Every year, college coaches are required to take an NCAA rules exam. Coaches are not allowed to recruit until they have successfully passed the test. This annual exam is just one example of how the NCAA changes its rules every year.

It is very important to understand the recruiting process has two functions with different meanings. These two functions impact how the coaches use their allotment of recruiting days.

1. Evaluation. A player has to be evaluated by a college coach before they can be considered a recruit. The initial evaluation is all focused on the individual player's skills.
2. Recruiting. This is the phase after an effective evaluation. Coaches devote the majority of their time both physically and mentally trying to convince players to attend their schools.

Coaches travel to evaluate or recruit a player but the focus needs to be on how coaches locate players to evaluate. Focusing on the NCAA's evaluation rules and calendar evaluation dates will give you the guidance for how coaches locate players. It is important to look at the NCAA rules from the coaches' point of view, because these rules are the blueprints they follow.

The Coaches' recruiting calendar is divided into two parts, Certified Events and Academic Year.

Certified Events

Certified Events are scheduled outside of a scholastic season and consist of two types of events; Travel Team tournaments and summer camps.

In the days before the rise of Travel Team play, the NCAA had very little interest or involvement in competition outside of the high school season. Over time, with the rise in the number of tournaments and teams as mentioned in the previous chapter, the NCAA set strict guidelines limiting the number of days college coaches could attend these events.

Since the inception of Travel Ball, college coaches have redefined how they go about using their time wisely locating prospects to evaluate. The most significant change came from coaches using NCAA Certified events to evaluate high school players, and no longer using the academic year to evaluate high school players.

Their reasoning was plain and simple; certified events gave the coaches the best opportunity to see as many kids as possible. A single tournament could have up to 75 sponsored teams, allowing one coach to see over 1000 players. With coaching staffs splitting up and covering different tournaments, this is ideal time of year to evaluate high school players.

Academic Year

The academic year calendar on paper is much the same since its inception, but what has changed is how college coaches go about using this time of year. It currently starts September 9 and goes through April 22, with certain dates in between specifying how coaches can use them.

The NCAA added one stipulation to the academic year recruiting rules. Coaches have a specific number of "person days." A "person day" is when a coach engages in an off-college campus recruiting activity of a prospective student-athlete. For example, if three coaches recruited on identical days they would be using three "person days." This allows coaches to randomly select their own days to recruit, but regulates everyone to ensure all have the same amount of days. Coaches are required to keep records on the players, dates and their "person days."

College coaches use the academic year now to concentrate on the recruitment phase of high school players. They also use this time to evaluate prep school and junior college players, knowing high school players are evaluated during certified events.

College Coaches Focus During Travel Team Tournament

The Travel Ball concept is the most popular way college coaches evaluate and locate high school prospects because they are able to see so many players in a short period of time. It is an ideal process to determine talent levels. Knowing how college coaches use this system today is a critical factor in understanding why your Travel Team participation may not lead to an evaluation.

This Travel Ball system has been invaluable to college coaches because it has eliminated most of the recruiting difficulties they experienced before Travel Ball.

1. College coaches no longer have to search for players to evaluate. Sponsored team coaches are spending their time and money finding and evaluating talent. College coaches attend certified events just to evaluate the players who have been recruited by a sponsored team.
2. The tournament format brings players to one location, which is ideal for evaluation.
3. The "best versus best" competition gives coaches a better opportunity to make good judgments when determining a player's potential.
4. Players are able to compete playing their correct position.
5. Rosters have underclassman.

This system has been in place for 30 years. Over time, with constant tweaking by the NCAA, coaches have had to adjust their approaches on how to use the system. The number of days' coaches are allowed to evaluate players has created the way they use the system to their benefit. With input from college coaches, the NCAA has created a calendar regarding when to schedule certified events.

NCAA recruiting calendar dates are shaped for Division I programs. Event orga-nizers schedule the largest events during this period. NCAA Division II, Division III and NAIA basketball programs also use this time to recruit heavily.

Understanding how college coaches use NCAA certified events to address their recruiting strategies and goals will have a great impact on a player's approach and strategies to getting evaluated. The limited number of days the college coaches have to recruit at these events requires them to come to each event with a previously devel-oped plan for their focus at the event. This plan includes how they will use their time, and on which players they will focus.

It is very important to remember college coaches have only eighteen days to eval-uate players as dictated by current NCAA rules for evaluation and recruiting. They must evaluate as many good players as possible during those days and that is why they focus on sponsored team rosters only.

While attending a certified event, a coach only has a short period of time and a sense of urgency to evaluate a very select group of players. This prevents the coach from randomly watching games, staying in one place for any length of time, and iden-tifying players not already on his or her list.

Coaches are also in the recruiting phase following players who they have already determined to be good enough. This visibility is the reason coaches at these events will wear polo shirts with their school name in big letters. Their time is also being used in evaluating underclassman so they can get a head start on recruiting future prospects.

College coaches very seldom evaluate players in a younger age bracket because the best underclassmen are usually found on 17U sponsored teams. A good example of coaches not attending anything but 17U events was the recruiting story of Louis Williams, a high school player from the Atlanta metro area. Louis was very good and played on a sponsored team, but he always played with his age group. He was very ca-pable at 14 years old to play on the 17U team. This would have given him tremendous exposure to college coaches.

When it came time for Louis Williams to play in 17U tournaments he was only known among local college programs who had been quietly recruiting him for years. College coaches were shocked as they watched Louis play for the first time the sum-mer before his senior year. They could not believe they did not know about him. Big time college basketball programs tried to get involved but Louis had committed to the University of Georgia because they had been recruiting him the longest. He never played in college. He was so talented he went straight to the NBA, drafted by the Philadelphia 76ers.

The different locations of certified tournaments and the few days in which to evaluate is the reason why college coaches cannot stay at one event to identify new talent. They need to utilize their time evaluating as many players as possible on sponsor team rosters that they have already put on their targeted recruiting list.

College coaches begin to prepare for these events during the winter months. By the end of February, the rosters of sponsored teams are finalized and their schedules completed. College coaches are in constant contact with these coaches. When I was recruiting students, I would communicate with as many as 30 coaches throughout the country, trying to locate possible prospects for the positions we were recruiting.

Sponsored team coaches are extremely important to college coaches because they are the initial source for information on a player. They have so much insight into who a player is and what their motivations are. This knowledge comes from time spent during tournaments with players, parents, relatives and friends.

When the Travel Team concept was embraced by the coaches to locate prospects, we never realized how this was going to impact high school basketball. The Travel Team season was now taking the place of a high school schedule, and the Travel Team coach gained credibility.

Bobby Cremins and I first realized this when we were visiting with Jamal Mashburn's coach, Tom Murray, in 1989. Jamal was a high school All-American at Cardinal Hayes in Bronx, New York.

Our initial visit to begin recruiting was with Coach Murray to explain why we were interested in Jamal. This was protocol. Without any hesitation, Jamal's Coach Murray, told us he was totally "out" of Jamal's recruiting. He recommended that we work through Jamal's Travel Team. This really caught us off guard because Tom was a friend and a well-respected coach in the City. We had consulted with him before when recruiting his players.

Misconception - The Benefit of Attending NCAA Certified Tournaments

While the NCAA controls all college coach recruiting activity, our entire youth sports landscape has some incorrect perceptions. The primary perception is that the Travel Team system plays the biggest role in getting a child "prepared" to get evaluated. It is also viewed as the best approach for exposure and getting a college coach's attention. I have already mentioned the Travel Team system alone will not improve individual skills for an evaluation. Now I will explain how the system works from a colleges coach's perspective concerning exposure and evaluations.

Coaches still use the Travel Ball system as their main source in evaluating high school players, but there are limitations and less time available for coaches because of the impact of NCAA rules on the coaches.

The misconception when it comes to playing in NCAA certified tournaments is the belief that playing on any team that participates in one of these tournaments is a sure bet to get your child evaluated by a college coach. Don't get caught in this trap.

The College Coach's Frame of Mind On the Recruiting Trail

Let's first connect you directly to what it is like for a college coach on a daily basis while on the recruiting trail.

The few recruiting days allowed by the NCAA each July is by far the most critical time to the college coach's success in recruiting. Coaches need to see as many of the best players as they can in any given state. During this time the following descriptions fit all coaching staffs, which should give you a good sense of why they remain focused on their strategy and current recruiting list.

1. Tense – this comes from the amount of mental pressure a coach feels during this crucial evaluation period due to limited time, the need to connect with recruits yet stay in touch with his or her current team situations back on campus.
2. Exhausted – traveling from one event to another in a short time period is overwhelming while also presenting diet and exercise challenges which adds stress for all coaches.
3. Connection Machines – as coaches evaluate players they are always trying to picture one recruit compared to another. At the same time, they are constantly trying to stay connected while listening to the "grapevines" of info about recruits and their possible interest in other schools.
4. Laser Focused – with very little time to evaluate a prospect, each live evaluation becomes so incredibly important and leaves no time for distractions or unplanned situations.

Having coached for a long time at the college level, I have created many friends and respected professional relationships. Trust me when I say most college coaches don't look forward to the summer recruiting period.

My annual mindset and schedule was always pre-programmed. I knew when practice started, season start and end dates, camp schedules and recruiting plans. We had little time for a family vacation. The schedule was the same year in and year out.

Evaluating and following prospects each summer was a time of year to which I never looked forward. Every year we had May and June off from any recruiting or evaluating of players. We used this time to plan where in July each member of the coaching staff was going. It usually began July 6 and ended on the 31st. For three weeks I would fly or drive from one city to another. Each day seemed like three because I would catch the morning session of games, have lunch, then attend the afternoon session followed by dinner and then back to the night session. This made for very long days.

The July schedule today has changed from what it was when I was coaching. Now it is only twelve days, broken up over the last three weeks in July, but the coaches are still using every minute in those days to their advantage.

A Typical Day on the Recruiting Trail

During the recruiting time of year, a typical day for me began with preparing the day's schedule before I left the hotel. Tournaments are usually set up in a 12-hour block of time. I could potentially watch 12 full games in a day. Very few coaches can ever watch that many games.

My daily plan included checking to see what players on my recruiting list needed to be seen for the first time along with those we were already recruiting, then match the players to their game schedule, checking the time and court they were playing on. If there was a conflicting game playing at the same time, I would split halves so I could see everyone I needed to.

I never randomly sat and watched games looking for new recruits if I had a break in my schedule. Depending on the time of day, I would eat lunch or dinner. I would also often return to the hotel to do office work and make calls to recruits. This is how all coaches handle their daily schedules.

Non-sponsored teams believe playing in the same events as the sponsored teams will afford the opportunity to be evaluated by many of the college coaches in attendance. This is not something to depend on. This belief by parents and players takes them down a path of spending time and money with little chance of getting on a college coach's radar.

A parent is rolling the dice when attending one of these events thinking the odds are in their favor for a college coach to evaluate their child. This does occasionally happen, but the small percentage of times it does is overblown and continues to support this myth throughout grassroots basketball.

Playing in the Travel Team system and participating in certified events has some benefits, but finding other approaches to get evaluated is a necessity, especially if your child is playing on a non-sponsored team to which college coaches are just not paying attention. Don't count on getting exposure and being evaluated by college coaches just because you are participating at an event they are attending. More effective strategies must be implemented if your child wants to play college basketball.

The harsh reality is that parents and players are seeing coaches at events, but these coaches already have their own agendas. The chances are extremely slim that they will notice your child unless they are already on their list.

Most parents and players believe playing on a Travel Team is the best way to get exposure. Unfortunately, this is not an accurate assumption if you play on a non-sponsored team. This belief eliminates thousands of American high school players annually from ever getting evaluated. Non-sponsored teams are not an effective focus for college coaches to address their recruiting needs and strategies.

If possible, college coaches would love the chance to evaluate more players. They just don't have the time, so they use the best approach they have, that of focusing on Sponsored Teams for their players.

NCAA Certified Camps

The NCAA treats summer camps the same way they do other events or tournaments: only select ones are certified.

Camps don't provide the exposure and evaluation opportunities they once did. There are many great camp operators who are good people and solid business owners. But the camps don't provide the exposure and evaluation opportunities they once did for players. Attendance by college coaches at these camps has been drastically reduced over the years. A key reason is that the players are staying with their Travel Teams and not attending camps.

With college coaches following the sponsored teams during this short recruiting period, the talent level at the summer camps is not what it used to be. This also has reduced the number of good instructional camps because young players are spending their time and money to play in certified tournaments. The chances are not very high that by attending a summer camp a player will be evaluated by a college coach.

In light of the tournament system and focus on sponsored team rosters being the main recruiting approach today, coaches may attend certified camps as a secondary strategy, but in small numbers.

College Coaches' Focus During the Academic Year

It is important to realize the old ways of how coaches recruited are no longer part of their business plan to locate prospects. Just because your child is a good high school player does not mean a college coach will evaluate him. The NCAA "Person Day" limitation is why assuming coaches will eventually see you play in high school is not a realistic plan.

The pressure to win that is put on college coaches today has drastically changed their philosophy on the type of player they recruit. Signing an experienced player has become the priority. This makes prep school, junior college and transfer players the main resources.

Transfer students are not recruited, but the recruitment of prep school and junior college players takes place during the academic year. This style of recruiting makes getting evaluated as a high school player even more difficult.

Coaches primarily attend high school games because they are in the recruiting phase trying to persuade a player to sign with them. College coaches may see your child play in high school, but they don't randomly attend high school games to find players. Coaches must strategically use these days. Very seldom are they used to evaluate a high school senior. These days are reserved for connecting with promising recruits, evaluating prep school and junior college players and following underclassman.

The perception that a college coach attends a high school game to identify and evaluate new players is understandable due to the fact that before Travel Ball, high schools were the main source for evaluating and recruiting. It is just no longer being done. Perception is NOT reality.

A key strategy when recruiting prior to Travel Ball was finding players we called a "sleeper." Sleepers were players who were under the radar, and not getting the attention they deserved because of the lack of time coaches could recruit. Locating sleepers defined how Bobby and I recruited years ago at Appalachian State University.

My first recruit I found was actually through a mistake I made. He was a big time sleeper. His name was Walter Anderson from New Hanover High School in Wilmington, NC. He was connected with Jimmy Hebron, a coach I knew from my high school days in New York.

In November, 1975, I was making my first trip to scout William and Mary, a Southern Conference opponent. I thought the game was at UNC-Wilmington. I drove seven hours from Boone to Wilmington directly to the college the day of the game. As I pulled up to the coliseum I got a bad feeling. The parking lot was empty. I was in the wrong place. UNC-Wilmington was playing William and Mary that night but the game was in Williamsburg, VA. This was my first assignment as a graduate assistant. It was a failure. Instead of driving directly back to Boone, I checked to see if there were any high school games scheduled in the area.

New Hanover high school had a home game, so before going home I decided to see them play. Immediately, I knew the point guard was a college player and assumed he was being heavily recruited. At the conclusion of the game, I visited with the coaches of New Hanover and realized I knew Jimmy Hebron, the JV coach from Queens, New York.

I met the head coach, Mike Brown, and commented on how good his point guard was. I asked who was recruiting him. He said his name was Walter Anderson, and he was getting very little attention from colleges. This was very surprising because my evaluation had him playing at a higher level than Appalachian.

I immediately called Bobby to tell him about my scouting mistake but mentioned I found a point guard to recruit. Bobby first thought recruiting a player seven hours away would be difficult but I responded by telling him how good he was. The following week Bobby saw him play and agreed with my assessment. This began my first recruiting assignment.

I drove twice a week to Wilmington, never spending the night, just to show Walter how much we wanted him at Appalachian. We eventually signed him. Walter Anderson started every game at Appalachian and was a key player in our success in winning the regular season title in 1978, and the Southern Conference Tournament Championship with a berth to the NCAA Tournament in 1979.

Finding "sleepers" like Walter does not happen today because of the system the college coaches use. Looking back on my initial evaluation of Walter, I assumed he was a level better than the Southern Conference. I had not recruited or coached a game in college at that point, but I can say now after all my years of recruiting experience that Walter Anderson was truly an ACC player.

Don't Let the Myths Fool You

I want to share my insights on some other myths you should not be hoping on to have a positive impact on your child's exposure and evaluation strategies. I am not saying a college coach will never locate a player because of these myths, but I want you to understand not to put a lot of confidence into these things. Don't weigh them heavily because they are not generally the way coaches locate players to evaluate today. Don't wait around hoping. All these illusions stem from the old ways coaches behaved in locating players.

1. <u>Individual Accomplishments</u> - The awards or accolades a player receives in high school are very special, but they do not get the attention of college coaches. It is just not possible for a college coach to evaluate every conference in every region of the country. (But do list them when creating an introduction sheet for prospective coaches. More on that in Chapter 23).

2. <u>Recognition such as Leading Scorer, Top Rebounder, Best Defender, MVP, All Conference, All Region, Regional All Star</u> – all these have no real impact on getting your child exposure, evaluated or recruited. These are common misconceptions as to what matters to a college coach.

3. <u>Team Accomplishments - Importance of Being on a Winning High School Team</u> - Many people believe that if their high school team is good, college coaches will notice. The truth is college coaches don't follow the records of high school teams throughout the country to find prospects. It is impossible to identify the nation's best players by using this philosophy. Coaches just don't have the time or resources to identify recruits this way.

4. <u>It Helps to Play High School Basketball with a Teammate Who's Being Recruited</u> - Coaches attending high school games have a heavy agenda as soon as they set foot on the high school's grounds. They are on a mission as a salesman to sign the player they are there to see. They will always be cordial and say the right things to anyone with ties to the high school program, especially parents of team members, because all the positive feedback the recruit gets on the coach's behalf could play into the decision on where the prospect goes to college.

Remember, a college coaches' recruiting list is very thorough. During the high school season, coaches have a laser focus to sign players from their list. While a coaching staff constantly updates its recruiting strategy, the high school season is part of the final stage in the recruiting process. A head coach and staff meet constantly about recruiting and have to manage a schedule with very little time for changes, constantly updating and strategizing their recruiting efforts with different tasks. They must also manage the status of where they stand with the recruits, scheduling phone calls, planning recruiting trips, setting up campus visits, the list goes on.

The final stage of a recruiting season includes the prioritized list of players by position and could consist of ten to thirty high school seniors. Adding an unfamiliar player to this list at this time would be very unusual because the NCAA recruiting calendar timeline is winding down. More importantly, this would disrupt their scheduled plan already in motion for recruiting players on their recruiting list. Coaches at this time of year are in their last leg of this annual long and grueling journey.

Non-Certified Events for Exposure

Over the last 15 years I have witnessed many different ways people and businesses are saying that they can assist and improve your child's chances of getting on a college coach's radar aside from a high school and Travel Team. All these different approaches come with a cost of valuable time and money. The determining factor in choosing to participate in any of these is to ask yourself, "will my child get evaluated by college coaches?"

One example is rating services. Rating services evaluating high school players were very popular before Travel Ball existed. These evaluators would watch high school teams and send out reports with a rating grade communicating the collegiate level of the player's skill set along with personal and school contact information such as height, weight, position and academics.

During my years coaching at Appalachian State (ASU), rating services for the most part became my main source in locating possible prospects. ASU is in Boone, NC, which is located in the Blue Ridge Mountains. There was a saying describing the location that "it takes two hours to get anywhere." So after learning how true that statement was, and spending a day's recruiting time evaluating prospects that were not good enough, back then I began to lean on rating service opinions before heading out of town.

The primary source of revenue for these rating or evaluation services was to charge a subscription fee to the college coach. Typically, the subscription was a weekly/monthly evaluation report on high school players throughout the country. These reports were expensive, but were very important to college basketball coaches and programs. Coaches justified the expense as saving time and money on wasted recruiting trips.

Before Travel Ball existed, college coaches used the high school season to evaluate and recruit players. This made these rating and evaluation services invaluable.

Evaluators assessed teams and players by personally watching them play. The original intent filled a huge need because college coaches were limited during a high school season when it came to finding players to evaluate.

Today coaches no longer depend on these rating services because sponsored team coaches do the initial evaluation. This evaluation system today is quick. It gives coaches opportunities to locate more prospects and provides college coaches a better opportunity to have a successful recruiting class. These certified events provide most of the evaluation insights college coaches need.

Today these rating services offer "evaluation and exposure clinics for players." These one or two day events typically promise all players will get exposure to college coaches attending the event and be evaluated. Receive a rating, which will be distributed to all colleges. These events are not NCAA certified because they are held during the non-evaluation period for Division I coaches. The colleges that are allowed to attend, NCAA Division II, III and NAIA I, II will normally be those that are located in close proximity to the event. When choosing to attend an exposure event, don't make your decision on wanting to get a rating because they are no longer used by coaches. Do it solely on the number of college coaches that will be attending.

Online Recruiting Services

Online recruiting services offer to contact the colleges on your child's behalf. They typically charge for personal information such as parent name, player name, address, phone, emails, parent's occupation, academic information such as GPA/test scores/ potential majors and basketball information such as high school coach's contact info, school address, accomplishments, videos and so on. Sending any of this information with a video is not something a coach will ask for. If it was part of the criteria coaches use to locate talent, this could certainly be done without the help of a recruiting service.

Coaches today do not evaluate players by watching videos because they have the opportunity to see thousands of kids play in person. Coaches are just not looking for a source to send them information and a video. It is not even on their radar. They simply don't have the time to watch them.

The approach coaches use to locate talent to evaluate is a very simple process. They don't complicate it by counting on all the different ways that the businesses throughout grassroots basketball in the US are creating to appeal to parents' and players' needs to get on a college coaches' radar!

There is a way to use a video to assist in getting on a coach's radar to evaluate your child which I will tell you later on how to use, but just sending random videos is not going to get the attention of a coach. Every year I was coaching I would get hundreds of videos sent to me. It was overwhelming. I had a routine in the spring to recycle the videos, knowing that they would continue to come in. I never took the time to watch them looking for a prospect.

Looking Back – Don't Do Things Just Because That's the Way It's Always Been Done

Another way to look at all this is to consider a historical view of the evolution of changes that have taken place in grassroots basketball. An understanding of history is a good way to help make decisions for what your child will face today, but it is always important to take into account what assumptions are no longer accurate today versus the past. Don't do things just because that is the way it has always been done.

Let's take a quick overview on the past in comparison to the reality of today. Before Travel Ball, coaches used numerous ways to find players, including high school games, practice, rating services, player accomplishments, media clippings/reports, summer camps, summer leagues, and word of mouth from coaches, alumni, friends and other community sources.

High school basketball is no longer an effective environment in which to evaluate players because it is tough to evaluate the depth of a player's skills when they are playing against fair talent. A high school team will rarely face opponents with other college bound players.

Another high school evaluation problem is that of players playing out of position because of the make-up of the team. Trying to imagine how they would play in their correct position adds a great deal of risk when making recruiting decisions.

As this new Travel Ball concept began to take shape in the late 80's, coaches realized this new format was an ideal way to find and evaluate players. This eliminated the old, time consuming way of doing things to locate players.

From the year 2000 to today, the NCAA rules have changed drastically concerning the way coaches could see as many teams as they wanted. Understanding these changes and the limitations they impose on the recruiting process for college coaches will give you the insights for making better decisions on how to leverage this system to get exposure and evaluation, and what will and will not work best for your child.

How many times have we heard that old story about cutting off the end of the ham?

A young woman was preparing a ham dinner. After she cut off the end of the ham, she placed it in a pan for baking. Her friend asked her, "Why did you just cut off the end of the ham"? And she replied, "I really don't know but my mother always did, so I thought you were supposed to."

Later, when talking to her mother she asked her why she cut off the end of the ham before baking it, and her mother replied, "I really don't know, but that's the way my mom always did it."

A few weeks later while visiting her grandmother, the young woman asked, "Grandma, why is it that you cut off the end of a ham before you bake it?"

Her grandmother replied, "Well, dear, otherwise it would never fit into my baking pan."

Keep in mind the moral of the story about cutting off the end of the ham as the decisions regarding how to leverage the Travel Team system to get exposure and evaluation from college coaches are made.

Youth parents and players have never focused on changes. They continued participating in a system with expectations that were no longer realistic due to the changing recruiting strategies of college coaches. They received little to no benefit for their time, effort and money spent, playing all the off-season games with the objective to improve, get evaluated and recruited.

Know why you are doing what you are doing. Don't do it because that is the way you have always done it, or everyone else has always done it. Do you cut off the end of the ham because that is the way it has always been done, or do you just buy a bigger baking pan? A different approach is what is often called for!

Despite the fact college coaches have totally embraced the Travel Ball system for their recruiting strategies, your child playing in this system does not mean that he or she is on the best path for getting the attention of college coaches. Don't just take the path that others are taking. It may not be the best approach for him or her, especially if your child is not playing on a Sponsored Team. There are other viable alternatives to increase your child's odds of playing college basketball.

Understanding sponsored teams versus non-sponsored teams gives an opportunity to consider if your child is on their best path. Chances are that if he or she is not on a sponsored team, you should be exploring different approaches if they want to play college basketball.

Keys to Remember

- Instead of using just the academic year for evaluating players, coaches shifted their focus to attending NCAA certified events.
- Realizing recruiting is the most important part of a coach's job should immediately focus a parent on the importance of understanding how coaches go about their business and not relying on the assumptions of others. The old ways of locating talent have completely changed, but many parents and players are still relying on those outdated scenarios.
- The key to putting the odds in your child's favor is to thoroughly understand how college coaches locate players to evaluate. It is also in being realistic about your child's level of talent so time isn't wasted having them go after unrealistic goals.
- Accomplishing the goal of being good enough to get on a college coach's radar and get evaluated will require a solid strategic plan.
- We are now into 30 years of Travel Ball, so most parents today don't understand there was any other system for off-season basketball in the US. It was not originally established as a new way to learn the fundamentals of the game and how to play basketball, but it has now taken over as the foundation of youth basketball in America.
- The change for college coaches was exciting because it opened up a new window on the calendar for them to identify college basketball prospects during the off season. The old way was packed into the academic school year, and made it tougher on the coaches because of all the conflicts they faced with their own team's season.
- Understanding that college coaches use sponsored rosters to evaluate high school players – and why – is critical as you consider the best strategies to get your child on a coach's radar for evaluation and recruiting.
- Academic year recruiting has totally been revamped since Travel Ball began. The myths of today were facts before Travel Ball existed. Coaches had to use all sorts of sources to find players which was more difficult in the past. With today's Travel Team system, they no longer waste valuable time with that approach.
- Player accomplishments, accolades, winning teams or playing with a college prospect have no impact on a college coach's approach to finding prospects today.
- The academic year is now strictly used for the final stages of recruiting by college coaches. Don't expect to get noticed by coaches during this time. It is not something to depend on for your child.

- The misconception abounds that playing on any team at a certified event will get your child evaluated by a college coach. This is just not true.
- These tournaments held during the live period are only beneficial to sponsored teams. Don't get caught up in all the hoopla surrounding these events if your objective is exposure and evaluation.
- Being in the same building with hundreds of college coaches attending might be exciting, but the reality of why these coaches are there needs to be faced. Expectations for playing in these off-season tournaments must be changed because they won't help your child get evaluated and recruited.
- NCAA certified *camps* are certified for one reason only: to be able to get coaches to attend which will enhance the number of participants. There is a slight possibility your child might be seen by a coach, but the number of coaches attending these camps is low because they have a better opportunity to see more potential prospects at an NCAA certified tournament.

CHAPTER 16

How College Coaches Recruit Players – The Decision Criteria

"Long range planning does not deal with future decisions but with the future of present decisions."
— Peter Drucker

have provided a lot of information throughout the chapters in this section to help parents better understand the exposure and evaluation "process." My goal is to share the history of how things evolved over the years. At the same time, I've tried to help you understand many of the assumptions about things throughout the grassroots basketball community that are not accurate when it comes to exposure and evaluation. I want you to have all the insights in order to make better and more informed decisions about how to address this very important area of navigating the right path for your child to play college basketball.

This chapter will focus on the specific criteria coaches use to make their decisions for players they want on their roster. Most parents and players never get the opportunity to talk with college coaches about how they create their recruiting strategy, and thereby rely on the myths that do not apply any longer.

When it comes to recruiting, the only opinion that matters is that of the college coach. Nothing can be more important than understanding how coaches make decisions from the perspective of the college coach, the person who will be deciding if your child will or will not fit the college basketball program's recruiting requirements.

The information in this chapter will enable you to see things through the eyes and mind of the college coach. This knowledge will enable you to create the strategies and make the decisions that will increase the odds of playing college basketball for your son or daughter.

Sponsored Team Rosters Are Key Drivers for College Coaches' Recruiting Schedule

The recruiting season is by far the most grueling time of year, with the NCAA rules only allowing college coaches six days in the spring and twelve days in the summer to evaluate NCAA certified events. So, the first priority in having a good recruiting season is accomplished by having a well-planned schedule so the staff can evaluate as many players as they can on the list.

As mentioned before, their schedule is built around the rosters of sponsored teams. Even though the priority is to locate and recruit rising seniors, coaches spend just as much time observing underclassman. These rosters have younger players playing up in age. A talented 14-year-old could also be playing on the 17U team. It is not unusual to see a roster of 15 with four or five underclassman competing.

To be successful in recruiting it is important to identify prospects as early as possible, so coaches are evaluating underclassman on 17U teams as much as they are evaluating rising seniors. Waiting to evaluate players until the summer before their senior year usually puts a coach in a tough position to sign him.

The NCAA rules allow colleges to communicate with players starting with the freshman class. The longer programs wait to contact prospects, the less the coach's chances are of signing a player. Coaches are always trying to get an edge to impress kids, and one of the keys is being able to say, "we were recruiting you first."

Managing the Recruiting List – Positions Needed

Coaches are always reworking and re-prioritizing their lists. Recruiting lists can be broken down into different categories in many ways. When I was recruiting, we had lists separated by grade. We segmented freshmen, sophomores and juniors. We had a main list consisting primarily of seniors. The list had underclassman on it if we had already determined them as future prospects.

As coaches prepare for a recruiting season, the first line of business are the roster positions needed. This immediately shrinks their recruiting lists, leaving only those senior players who fit their needs.

The underclassmen listed players in all positions because we could never fully predict our needs.

Roster Limitations

Coaches have limitations on how many players they can have on a roster. The number of roster spots are determined by NCAA/NAIA rules or the individual schools. For example, NCAA Division I schools only allow thirteen men's and fifteen women's scholarship players.

Positions typically are decided by the current makeup of players on the roster who are in their last year of college eligibility. For example, if a coach has a senior point guard starting and the backup is a junior, he recruits a point guard. This would allow the freshman point guard to be backup for one year.

The primary reason a coach recruits by position is to ensure he always has a player with college playing experience starting. They want to stay ahead of the game to avoid having to be too dependent on freshmen. The difficulty freshmen have when competing their first year is the physical aspect of the game. You have to remember they are 18 or 19 years old and are competing against players who might be 22 years old. There are exceptions, but most need time to adjust.

Coaches also look for players who are capable of playing more than one position. Trying to recognize other determining factors that play into their evaluation is always on their minds. This is a tremendous bonus for coaches. This is equivalent to getting two players for one.

Labeling positions have changed from the original five position thinking. It used to be point guard/one man, shooting guard/two man, small forward/three man, strong forward/four man, center/five man. Coaches, for the most part, now break it down into three categories: point guard, perimeter and bigs.

The only position that is difficult to use in another position is a point guard. A point guard can play another position on the perimeter, but it is hard for a perimeter player to play point guard. It is still a unique position that takes years of experience. It is hard to make someone a point guard in college who has not played for a number of years before getting to the college level. Experience at this position is a key to becoming a legitimate point guard on the college and pro level.

During the Bobby Cremins era at Georgia Tech, the recruiting world gave us the name "Point Guard U." It all started with Mark Price followed by Craig Neal, Kenny Anderson, Travis Best and Stephon Marbury. All went on to play in the NBA.

During Travis Best's career, Drew Barry was also a very good point guard but he started at the off guard position. Travis brought the ball up the court and got us into the offense. Then, Drew's point guard skills took over, controlling our team in the half court set.

The talk in the NBA about Drew was that he was a possible first round draft choice. He was invited to Phoenix to participate in a showcase for possible NBA prospects to prove himself as a point guard. I watched Drew for three days during this showcase. He played well in the half court set, but struggled when pressured full court.

He very seldom brought the ball up the court and got us started into our offense during his years at Georgia Tech. His performance at the showcase immediately changed how he was looked upon as an NBA prospect. Drew did play in the NBA but not having the total guard experience in college shortened his career.

Recruiting Formula

As coaching staffs begin to evaluate players, they will rework their lists, eliminating many because of information they observed or received while doing their due diligence on players. A coaching staff will constantly ask these questions throughout the recruiting process while evaluating players:

1. Is the player good enough for us?
2. Is he interested in our program?
3. Is he a good student?
4. Is he a good person?

Are You Good Enough?

The head coach wants his staff to observe the same player at different times just to make sure of their decision. After evaluations, some players on the list are not good enough. Making these decisions are critical because to continue to recruit a player that eventually the coach realizes is not good enough translates into wasted time and money for them.

Players are characterized as athletic, skilled, or athletic and skilled. The Travel Ball system changed how coaches evaluate players. This system has produced a certain style of player, redefining how coaches evaluate players.

The Travel Team system places the game as the primary learning tool regarding how to play basketball. This has had a major impact on the skill level of American players. The lack of individual skills such as footwork, ball-handling and shooting, have turned the coaches' focus to other things when evaluating and finding the best athlete.

Athletic players stand out from most because they are exciting to watch, but not necessarily because of skill talent. They are gifted physically. Obviously it can be seen in their jumping ability, but the speed they show getting up and down the floor, along with their lateral movements on defense stands out. Their creativity in taking shots is also easy to see. Coaches now base their decisions when evaluating players in the Travel Ball system on how much he can "wow" them, which is all based on athleticism. The athletic player has always had a spot on the college level, but prior to the Travel Ball system they were not a coaches' first choice. The skilled player was more valuable in the past.

The skilled player can take on a higher value in the recruiting process, but it will require changing the approach for this type of player to get on a coach's radar and get evaluated. This is where opportunity for your child increases if you follow the strategies I have shared with you throughout this book. Skilled players are a totally different breed of player. These players lack the explosiveness of an athletic player, but make up for it in so many other ways. Their attributes vary from being a shooter, ball handler, passer, having great instincts or having tremendous knowledge of the game.

I had a reputation as a recruiter for signing players that were not highly rated. I favored recruiting the skilled player. It took time because it might take a number of evaluations before I could recognize all of a player's qualities. One key ingredient was a must for me: a perimeter player had to be a good shooter. This type of player will not be noticed by a sponsored team coach, not because of their knowledge in finding players like this, but because these kinds of players just don't fit their game plan and system.

Sponsored Travel Team coaches, for the most part, will recruit players who can play in a wide-open system. There is limited time to practice, which means this style is dominated by athleticism over team play. Each player has his own agenda for how he displays his talents.

The three decades of Travel Ball have drastically decreased the number of skilled players coming out of high school. This has left the college game, for the most part, with only American players who are athletic.

There was a time when conferences were labeled by their style of play. The Big East was a league of tough players. The ACC was a league of skilled players with good guard play. The SEC was a league of athletic players.

Travel Ball tournament games are fast and feature full court trapping defenses and offenses defined by fast breaks. The athletic player can show his positive attributes almost every trip down the court either offensively or defensively. The fundamentally sound basketball-intelligent player is limited as to how he can show his skills in this type of game.

There was a fascinating story in *Sports Illustrated* in the March 9, 2015 edition that supports my explanation on how coaches evaluate Travel Team basketball. The story was about Jeff Teague (Wake Forrest) who played point guard for the Atlanta Hawks and now is with the Indiana Pacers, and how he has come full circle. He was first taught to play the game unselfishly by his dad, and then became a selfish player in order to get recognized by college coaches, but then he returned back to what he learned from his dad.[4]

His dad played at Boston University for Rick Pinto. Rick took his scoring mentality as a point guard and transformed his game into a true point guard, dishing out 633 assists in three seasons. His dad took this knowledge and instilled it into his young son, Jeff, teaching him how he could become an effective point guard. For example, when Jeff started playing in high school, it was important for him to memorize where every starter was positioned on every play. Jeff learned to feel success through his unselfish approach when all the players on his team finished with 10-12 points a game.

Jeff started with this same philosophy when playing on the number one Travel Team in Indiana. He was teamed up with future NBA players Eric Gordon, Mike Conley, Greg Oden and Josh McRoberts. There was one major problem as Jeff entered his second summer playing Travel Ball and using his unselfish play to make his teammates better. The others were all getting recruited heavily, but Jeff had nothing.

He and his father realized something had to change to get coaches to see he was athletic and capable of scoring. He decided to become a more selfish player, forgetting about distributing the ball and being the athlete he was taught to be. Jeff went on and signed with Wake Forest where he continued to play with this new philosophy. After his sophomore season he was drafted 19th by the Atlanta Hawks (2009).

Nothing changed in Jeff's style of play until 2013 when the Hawks hired Mike Budenholzer, a long time assistant with the San Antonio Spurs. To fully understand

4 Lee Jenkins, *Sports Illustrated*, March 9, 2015, Doing Their Fair Share

this story, it is important to know the San Antonio Spurs offensive philosophy. The Spurs, who have won five NBA titles under Greg Popovich, are a team that moves the ball quickly, not allowing one player to have it too long. All players must play unselfishly.

This mentality was not a hard transition for Jeff, and in 2015 he became an All Star. In the playoffs his style of play was solidified when beating the Nets with 13 assists and no points. He is now considered one of the top 50 players in the league. This story is not about college coaches and their offensive philosophy because they all teach moving the ball. It is about the style of play in Travel Ball and the impact it has on how coaches evaluate Travel Ball players.

Coaches have no control over the way teams play, so they concentrate on the individual areas of the game that players exhibit the most. The two biggest concentrations are athletic ability and capability of individually scoring.

Another reason for the wide-open style of play in these tournament games is the lack of a scouting report for opposing teams. For example, if a team goes up against a full court zone press without any real practice time, they break the press by athleticism. Without the athleticism, the team doesn't stand a chance competing in these situations.

The biggest impact all the off-season playing of games has had on American youth basketball is that the non-athletic kids are not becoming skilled. They are spending too much time playing games and not improving their skills. It is important to understand that just because your child does not show the athleticism of others, it does not mean his days are numbered playing basketball.

The real issue is that because kids in the US have not been working on their individual skills, it is rare to see enough players with good skills competing with athletes. This is the reason so many college roster spots are occupied by foreign players, and proof that college coaches want more of these types of players. They are taught the skills to compete on the highest levels, regardless of how athletic a player is. There is an opportunity for more players in the US to get the attention of college coaches and be recruited to fill a college roster spot. The way to do this is to focus more on individual skill development to increase their odds of playing college basketball.

Are You Interested in Their Program?

It is important for coaches to learn information about the player's interest in their program. They don't want to waste time and money on players with a low probability of signing them. Contacting players on their list is very important before they set up their recruiting schedules. Getting answers to these questions are all done within NCAA guidelines allowing telephone calls or personal visits to the high school.

I could write a book on players we recruited for years starting their freshman year in high school only to find out that when they decided on where they would attend college, their interests had changed. Some of those decisions were a total shock to us because we did not see it coming. It was the toughest part of the business.

There are three players that come to mind regarding a change of interest: Shareef Abdul Dehiam, Damien Wilkens and Al Harrington. All three are good guys and had successful NBA careers, but the time and energy we spent with them made it a hard pill to swallow when they decided not to attend Georgia Tech. Shareef and Damien chose colleges away from Atlanta, and Al declared for the NBA right out of high school. I have always blamed myself for not knowing their changing interest. If we had known, our time could have been spent on other prospects.

Are You a Good Student?

Coaches need this information as soon as possible so they don't waste time recruiting players. As they gather names for the evaluation season, this is a crucial question in their due diligence. The most reliable source is the high school coach. They have access to the player's transcripts. Travel Team coaches might have pieces, but not all the facts.

Are You a Good Person?

Is the player a good person with the right values? This is so important to college coaches. They take this evaluation as seriously as any other. After determining an athlete's basketball skills are good and has good grades, the next important factor to learn is whether they fit into the culture of the coach's team. How do they interact with their parents, and how do they treat their classmates and teachers? Coaches need positive players to help promote and ensure a positive atmosphere.

Key to Remember

- It is important to learn how college coaches go about their business of recruiting because what is perceived by our youth basketball system is way off course. How coaches locate players to evaluate is crucial because the majority of kids are on the wrong path simply because they are not paying attention to how coaches operate.

- College coaches use sponsored teams as their main source in evaluating high school players. If your child is not on one of these teams, the chances of being evaluated playing Travel Ball are not good.
- Another important understanding in the evaluation process is the coach's need to determine the positions they will be recruiting. Coaches have limitations on the number of players they can have on a roster, which plays a factor in how many players each year they can recruit.
- The formula coaches go through in the evaluation process does not stop at a player's playing ability. The player's interest in their program, academics, and the type of person a player is all play a key part in the evaluation process.
- Knowing the drivers behind the coach's recruiting strategy will help you create the best approach and decision criteria to navigate the path to increase the odds for playing college basketball.

Be sure to access bonus content as my gift to you

www.KevinCantwellBasketball.com/p/gifts

SECTION 5

Parents - Your Role in Your Child's Success

"Parents are the ultimate role models for children.
Every word, movement and action has an effect.
No other person or outside force has a greater
influence on a child than the parent."
— BOB KEESHAN

The youth sports community on a whole is telling parents to let go and stay uninvolved as it relates to their child's participation in a sport. "Everyone" is talking about the behavior of parents and how they need to get out of the way because they are overinvolved.

Parental behavior is important and must be addressed, but I believe there is even a bigger issue of which parents need to be more mindful. I believe parents need to GET *MORE* INVOLVED. The key is to do it in the right way.

Parents need to extend their parenting role into youth basketball and NOT just become a spectator. Knowing how to do that is key. Parents becoming more involved means knowing when to take the lead on something, when to follow someone and when to let go and get out of the way. Doing all three things well will enable you to actively and effectively manage the youth basketball system in the US for your child's benefit, thus successfully extending the parenting role.

A descriptive analogy of this would be knowing when to drive a car, when to become a passenger and let someone else drive, and when to get out of car. This is the key to navigating the youth basketball path in the best interest of your child, the key to keeping your child on the road and out of the ditch. It's the only way to manage the imperfect youth sports system. Your child will end up on the side of the road if you leave it up to others (the system) to steer the car.

The youth basketball system is not set up to manage things for your child in a comprehensive way. It's no different than other things in society where services are provided, but we have to take the responsibility for managing them. A good example would be our own healthcare system. We can't become doctors, just as all parents can't become basketball coaches. We need the doctors and other fine professionals along with services provided by the healthcare infrastructure, but we have to play a role in managing our own care.

Parents and players need so many of the good, well-meaning people in the youth basketball system, but the system is just not set up for any one person to manage your child's journey in a comprehensive way. The role has to be played by you. It's no different than the parenting role you play as you oversee and manage the other areas of your child's life as they grow up. One day you will let them go as they move into adulthood. Why should youth basketball be any different?

All you need to oversee and manage the basketball process for your child is to seek the knowledge and guidance to address these five things:

1. Clarity for what your role is and how to play it effectively.
2. Learn enough about how the youth basketball system works.
3. Understand the parts of the system that will work for your child and what parts won't.
4. Gain access to the right expert resources to guide and coach you along your journey.
5. Gain access to the right expert resources to work with your child.

The above five things will allow you to make the right decisions as to when you need to drive the car, when you need to move into the passenger seat and when it is okay to get out of the car.

Reaching Section 5 of this book has already given you a solid foundation for so much of the above five things. This last section will give you some final pieces. Knowing more specifically the role you need to play in supporting your child will enable you to focus on all the right things to ensure your child reaches maximum basketball potential.

CHAPTER 17

"Team" Coach – You Need Realistic Expectations

"Only one who devotes himself to a cause with his whole strength and soul can be a true master. For this reason, mastery demands all of a person."
— ALBERT EINSTEIN

I feel the title of "coach" is very special, and not because it was my profession, but due to the incredible hard work and experience that goes into getting that title. In the medical profession after years of schooling, studying and practical experience, a person is given the title, "doctor." An expert coach goes through many parallel specified sports journeys to acquire the title, "coach."

The challenge in youth sports is that volunteers are needed to take on the job of coaching. Many of these are parents or other well-meaning people contributing their time to support youth sports. They don't have the depth of knowledge and experience to be accountable and held to the same standards as experienced high school, college or pro coaches.

Outside of the United States, most youth programs require their coaches to become certified in the sport they are teaching. If a coach is not certified, they are not given the coaching title but are referred to as "Mr." or "Ms."

We would not critique a doctor in surgery because we do not understand what it takes to operate. Coaching should be treated with the same respect. If parents understood the coaching profession, they would find it so much harder to critique a team coach.

The qualifications to be given the title of "coach" are very difficult. Coaching, like any other professional job, requires a person to love what they do and at times put dedication to the role ahead of other high priorities in their life.

Coaching is an occupation performed in the public eye. This allows many people to feel that they have the ability to evaluate, judge and criticize a coach's performances effectively. It is a job where your effectiveness is measured on winning and losing. As a professional coach, being judged by others can be frustrating at times, but is an accepted critical part of the job. Hall of Fame Coach John Wooden once said, "If you cannot handle the exterior don't get into coaching."

What It Takes to Be a Good Coach –Volunteers Don't Have the Time

The majority of a coach's work is in preparing to put all the pieces together. It is done out of the public eye. It took a few years when I started my coaching career before I realized how much work had to be done to have a successful team.

A coach's team objective every season is to have chemistry. Players have to believe in the system. They all must understand their roles. This is easier said than done because the formula to achieve chemistry goes way beyond the basketball court. Some teams can achieve it, and others struggle. It is dependent on the mindset of individual players.

If only the mixture on how to achieve chemistry could be bottled up! Team or business success would be so much easier. Teams that have chemistry are fun to coach because the players know what to do individually, and know how their contribution impacts the team as a whole. The coaching time and effort that goes into getting players to think in unison is exhausting but the rewards are enjoyable and every coach's dream.

The 1990 Georgia Tech team had the best chemistry of any team I ever coached. We won the ACC tournament and followed that with four more wins in the NCAA tournament. The ultimate chemistry game was our fourth win, beating Minnesota in the Superdome, advancing us to the Final Four in Denver. The final score was 93-89.

Three of our players, Kenny Anderson, Dennis Scott and Brian Oliver, had 89 of the 93 points, but that is not why we won. We had three other players who played. Their offensive statistics gave us the victory. Malcolm Mackey played 24 minutes and took no shots. Johnny McNeil played 26 minutes, scored 2 points, and was 1 for 1 from the field. Karl Brown played 30 minutes, scored 2 points, and was 1-3 from the field. In

80 minutes of play these three players took a total of four shots. This was chemistry at its best. Everyone knew their role.

These players contributed tremendously, but they knew taking shots was not what was best for the team. Think about this. Let's just say Malcolm and Johnny decided to take one more shot a piece. This would be understandable for the amount of minutes they played. But if they missed, we would have lost the game and not have our Final Four memories.

These three players went on and had successful professional careers in Europe because they understood they could contribute in so many other ways outside of scoring. All three were excellent defenders and rebounders. They unselfishly set great screens along with being good passers.

To be an effective coach, a lot of personal contact time with players is needed off the court so success can be achieved on the court. A coach's job off the court consists of:

1. Getting players to believe in themselves. Building self-esteem so they will continue to improve. Staying away from embarrassment, humiliation or playing head games that leave the player questioning their ability.
2. Teaching life skills beyond the X's and O's. Looking for opportunities to teach important lessons such as mastering hardship, handling failure and setbacks, trusting teammates, sacrificing individual needs for the benefit of the group, emotionally dealing with winning and losing, good sportsmanship, honesty and integrity.
3. Understanding their players are different in attitude, personality, ability, sensitivity and how they handle adversity. Time must be spent getting to know each player's differences. This is critical to gaining their trust.
4. Understanding all of your player's emotions. The last person on the team is as important as the best player. This is another way of getting loyalty among the players.

If a person is not able to cover all of these critical aspects of coaching, they are a coach in name only.

Coaches don't coach teams. They teach and coach individuals—the team aspect is just putting in a basketball system.

Teaching players a team system or philosophy is very time-consuming and extremely intense because coaches are working towards the finished product that the public will critique.

Another perception of coaching is thinking that individual skill work and preparing to play games can be achieved at the same time. The season is strictly for teaching the complexity of each specific team philosophy, getting players to learn offenses, out of bounds plays, special situations and defensive philosophies. Watching game videos and preparing the team for the next opponent is extremely time-consuming. Practicing five to six days a week is not an easy task. Working on team chemistry and giving players their specific roles doesn't just happen overnight.

My biggest frustration when attending a high school or a Travel Ball game is watching kids try to do things on offense they are not capable of doing. The key to any player's game is knowing their role. Knowing your role is having a good understanding of your strengths and weaknesses.

Players need someone other than themselves to assess their strengths and weaknesses because typically they believe they can do almost anything during game situations. As a game begins, I usually see the strengths of most players quickly. In my own mind I identify their role. As the game progresses players consistently go outside of their comfort zone attempting to do things they cannot do. Most players throughout grassroots basketball do this because they are playing so many games without the proper personal instruction for what their role should be.

The frustrating part of coaching is an entire season can go by with some players never grasping parts of what is being taught. I can remember a situation while coaching at Georgia Tech where we were upset on the road while playing Richmond. They played a zone defense the entire game.

After the game I went to get something to eat with Rick Barry, one of our players' parent. Rick is one of the greatest player to ever play in the NBA. His son, Jon, had a long career in the NBA, and now works as an ESPN NBA analyst. Jon was in his first season at Georgia Tech.

Rick Barry and I were dissecting the game and Rick started using sugar packs to show me a good zone offense. He moved the packs from place to place showing specific movements required for making an effective offense. I told him that what he was showing me was very similar to what we were trying to accomplish in our zone offense. The difference was that the sugar packs didn't have personalities and minds of their own.

So, why do I take the time to tell you all these things about what it takes behind the scenes to build a team? As you critique your child's Travel Team coach, or any one of the team coaches for that matter, be very realistic about your expectations.

There are a lot of good people who dedicate their time to coaching youth basketball, but they are volunteer people who do other things for a living. Don't lose sight of what your expectations should be. Don't expect them to do the same things full-time, experienced coaches can do.

Team coaches have very little time to correctly prepare players and teams for competition. Playing more than one game a day is not possible for which to adequately prepare. Coaches struggle to find practice facilities. They typically practice no more than twice a week, and there isn't any film or scouting sessions to help in the process.

Travel Team coaches spend so much time with your child. This creates the perception that the coach is the key person in your child's basketball development. He is not only coaching your child's games, but is responsible for improving your child's individual skills.

I have listened and watched parents complain about coaches for different reasons. They often decide to change teams only to find out "the grass is not any greener on the other side." The problem lies in your expectations of coaches. So often those expectations are not realistic.

Bobby Cremins was a player's dream for a coach. I had the distinct honor to work with him for 20 years. He taught that treating players as people came first, and caring more about them personally. It was important to take an interest in their life outside of basketball. These factors of coaching are extremely important because this is how coaches get players to trust and respect them. Without this a coach will not be taken seriously when communicating.

After about ten years of working with Bobby, I figured out the ingredients to becoming a successful college coach. My formula was "60/30/10." 60% was all about recruiting. A team cannot win without good players. 30% was about getting the trust and respect of the players recruited, which on the average, took at least a year to develop. 10% was about the X's and O's.

I have passed this message on to so many young college coaches. I've told them not to spend the majority of time with team basketball philosophy. Instead, get to know their players as people. This is done by being concerned about their lives outside of basketball. I talk to high school coaches with the same message, understanding that recruiting, for the most part, is not feasible for them. I tell them the priority should be to get close to their kids.

When looking at my 60/30/10 formula, team coaches struggle to get high marks in any of the areas because of the time restraints they have. Recruiting is limited. They don't have the time and situations to work on trust. The basketball philosophy and team system is a struggle because of the lack of practice time needed to get all the players on the same page playing as a unit.

As I described previously in this book, Travel Ball competition is a form of an organized pickup game. You have a representative as a coach, but this person has very little time to mold the players into a team. Holding them responsible to improve your child's individual skills is not realistic or fair to them. It is impossible for them to be accountable for the development of your child's individual skills.

As someone who has done this for a long time, I must admit developing your child to consistently improve is a very complex process, and one that requires someone with professional knowledge and expertise.

The world of Travel Ball has become such an off-season emphasis in our current youth sports system that in the minds of parents and players, these volunteer coaches are often believed to be more important than high school coaches. This is due to many factors such as college coaches use of the Travel Ball system for their evaluation and recruiting, amount of games played, weekend tournament atmosphere, and so forth. There are good people who volunteer their time to coach in the system. I just want you to have realistic expectations for the outcomes you seek from them.

Key to Remember

- As a parent, realize you can't expect youth coaches to take care of all your child's basketball development. Volunteers who are given the name "coach" do not automatically change a coach's qualifications.
- Basketball practices have two purposes:
  - Team practices concentrate on preparing players to work as a unit when competing; and
  - Individual practice is honing in on skills and repetitions.
- Volunteer coaches are typically focused on team practices. Because of the lack of time required to get players to play together, playing as a team is almost impossible. This leaves little time for individual practices to focus on skill development in off-season basketball.
- Understanding the criteria for a coach to meet to be successful should change the focus from depending on volunteers to give your child the necessary tools for skill development. You need to identify other resources in your local area for this assistance.

CHAPTER 18

How Significant is the Coach?

*"I just think we should not get into counting coaches' records.
I've never been for that... but I know that's just American society."*
— DEAN SMITH

When playing a team sport, there are many people a parent and child must take into consideration. Teammates, other parents and officials, are important, but the most important person is their coach. No matter what type of coach, volunteer, school or college coach, they are the ones who make the decisions that can personally influence your experience.

One of the ways a parent can harm their child is by not being careful about how the relationship with a coach is managed throughout your child's basketball journey. All coaches will have different philosophies and do things differently in their own way, even with the decisions they make concerning your child. Remember what goes into making a coach should lower your expectations and keep you supportive.

Parents need to stay the course and not involve themselves in the coaches' responsibilities or decisions. Let your child speak for himself with his coaches. It helps him mature in learning that he must be responsible and accountable for and to his own relationships. It also demonstrates the need to learn that life will not always go his or her way. Your child needs to learn how to manage those situations on their own.

Academically, parents will be more involved with their child's teachers. But because it is your child's choice to play basketball, letting your child act on his or her own behalf is giving him or her your respect. It also helps them learn how to deal with an authority figure in their life on their own. This is no different than when they get older and must build a relationship with their boss and learn to manage conflicts that will naturally surface at given points in time.

Coaches are sensitive like anyone else. Just because their decisions are public knowledge does not mean it is okay to be judgmental about them. Coaches on all levels have a common understanding that they are going to be scrutinized, but those parents who take it too far are very well known among coaches.

A parent's reputation within coaching circles will have an impact on how much another coach will want their child playing for him. The impact will be either positive or negative. You have full control over whichever it is. If parents were in a position to hear the honest views of coaches, they would tell the parents the majority of negativity they face coaching below the college level comes from them!

It isn't worth the risk of having a negative encounter with a coach over any situation. Don't pick a battle because it will almost certainly lose you the war. Parents have reputations in all the coaching circles. The reputation is passed onto other coaches. These coaches may be potential coaches of your child in the future.

Parents' reactions to coaching can be damaging to their child at any age. When my son was ten he was trying out for a local recreation league team. Everyone trying out was going to make a team, but the tryouts were evaluations because the coaches were going to pick their teams in a draft. I was good friends with most of the coaches, so they let me sit in on the draft.

I was amazed hearing the coaches express their feelings regarding why they would not pick certain players. They were all based on the actions of the player's parents! I specifically remember the three best players kept getting overlooked until eventually a coach had to take them. The sad part about this story is that the parents were a major topic in a rec league draft with ten year-olds! The parents were never even aware how their child was being blamed for *their* actions.

Over the years I have listened to middle and high school coaches commenting about some players and their parents. They would talk about how the behaviors of the parents were slowly ruining their child's opportunity for success with basketball. Most coaches were surprised to hear when I told them we were dealing with identical issues on the college level also.

College coaches understand freshman are learning a completely different environment their first year of college than the one they grew up around. They are always curious about their new coaches and the level of trust they can have with them. It sometimes takes one whole year for the coaching staff to gain their trust and respect. This is a natural situation with all new players. Having parents who question the coach's decisions all the time makes it tough on their child to make his or her own decisions about trusting the coaching staff.

We had a very talented young man who was very close to his parents and was always respectful to our staff on and off the court. During practice he would listen, giving us every indication he bought into what we were teaching him. When the game started it was like he never practiced, always taking shots he was not capable of making at a high percentage.

We knew what was happening because his parents would give us hints from time to time about how he needed to score more points. We had hoped the parents would eventually buy into what we were teaching their son, but they never did.

The victim in all of this was their son. He had the potential to have a good NBA career but had a short pro career in France. Even though he was a starter for his entire college career, he showed very little improvement over his four years. He never could totally trust the coaching staff and what we were trying to do to develop him as a player. His parents, who were great people, wanted him to do things their way. I truly believe his parents had their son's best interest at heart and thought they were doing what was right. Getting conflicting reports on how to do something is very confusing and hinders the improvement process.

The most interesting story of parent involvement I have heard was told to me by a well-known general manager in the NBA. This GM was a friend of mine. I asked him about a player on his team. The player was a great kid. I recruited him for a short time at Georgia Tech, but made a decision to stop solely based on one of his parents.

In our conversation I told him why I stopped recruiting this player. The GM told me about a confrontation he had had with this one parent. The player was a rookie and not getting a lot of playing time. This led to the parent expressing their opinion to the GM on how his son should be playing more. The GM got so frustrated he finally said, "Okay, if you don't like what is going on, we can tear up his contract immediately." The contract was worth approximately four million dollars.

College coaches seek to learn as much as they can during their evaluation process of a player. They will focus on a player's family life and the levels of involvement parents have in supporting their child. How parents involve themselves in their child's basketball life is very important to coaches. When a player is totally clear-minded and not having input from the outside on how they should play, improvement comes quickly. The player will have a greater chance of realizing his or her potential.

As I reflect on my own time recruiting players, our coaching staff always talked about our recruit's parents when doing our due diligence. One of the initial questions we always asked was, "how are the parents?" It was critical for us to learn how a recruit's parents behaved and handled themselves during and after games. This was such an important concern because parents who don't completely trust their child's coaches will slow the developmental process down.

High school coaches can be an influential part of your child's college basketball decision. Be careful to never undermine your child's coach. Subtle, passive aggressive comments like, "Your coach doesn't know what he is doing," or, "I can't believe you don't play more," fosters an environment of bad attitudes and decisions.

High school coaches are in a better position to evaluate your child and make the appropriate basketball decisions just as his or her teachers are in the academic classroom. Coaches observe the workouts, practices, meetings, and film sessions. The parents are not there and don't have all the information the coach has about their child. The child and the coach are really the only two people needed to talk thru any issue that arises.

Parents want their child's coach to work hard for them, not against them, when the time comes when college coaches are reaching out to learn as much as they can about their child and family. So do not allow your behaviors to get in the way of this.

Remember, when somebody believes strongly in something, the sales pitch can be off the charts. A child's high school coach will go out of his way to promote the player if he has been treated with respect during the child's time with him.

I have attended an unbelievable amount of elementary, middle and high school games. I have found that there is a relationship between a child's ability to play and parent behavior. The more talented kids have parents who see their child's potential, so they get involved with constant critiquing. But regardless of the level of play, when parents are negative and/or overinvolved, coaches will subconsciously make decisions concerning your child that will not play out in his or her favor.

Key to Remember

- You need to realize every coach along the journey is important. They are making decisions concerning your child so negative behavior or over involvement by you could impact their judgment.

- Understand parents on all levels are being evaluated; pre-high school, high school and college.
- Every coach will be a great resource for you, not because of their basketball knowledge or lack of it, but as your child's supporter as they move on to the next level team.

CHAPTER 19

Take Ownership. Know When to Lead and When to Let Go.

"It is not what you do for your children,
but what you have taught them to do for themselves,
that will make them successful human beings."
– ANN LANDERS

Your child choosing basketball as "their" sport is an exciting time. Parental guidance is so critical to a positive experience and their success because of the misconceptions in our youth system about what is best for learning and finding the edge to excel.

Kids do not usually express their dreams of playing in college or the pros, but I guarantee your child has those aspirations. He or she needs your help to reach for them. It is so important to learn how to "reach for" our goals just as it is to learn how to deal with success when we attain it, or how to cope with not getting what we want.

Your child does not have the ability to understand all the challenges to their goals and dreams they face throughout their participation in the sport. These challenges are compounded because of the many misconceptions about the best path to take to improve and make teams at the next level throughout their years of playing basketball.

It is not as easy as following what other parents and kids are doing. I have already explained many of them are choosing paths driven by the myths or misconceptions about what it takes to excel in playing basketball.

A challenge parents will face is how to support their child without taking ownership away from them for the goals they themselves choose to reach during their time playing the game. He or she cannot succeed without you playing the RIGHT ROLE, and playing it well.

Initially, parents have to agree that the road most traveled by others participating in the sport is not always the best path for your child. This can only be accomplished if parents first understand the things in the system your child should not be following. Through your newfound knowledge brought out by reading this book, create the right path for your child, and help them understand what is best for them.

Guiding Behind the Scenes and Doing What is Right

As a parent, you need to think of your role as one that is "behind the scenes," consulting and assisting inside the family circle. At the same time, stay away from getting involved with decisions being made by others about your child's skills.

It is so important for parents to put all their mental energy into being their child's role model and leading by example. Staying clear of all the commenting and questioning that goes on when playing team sports. Teaching your child to stay focused on themselves rather than blaming others is a huge task, and can only be accomplished with parental guidance.

Your child cannot reach their goal without your help. At the same time, not playing the right role and going about things in the wrong way will work against them succeeding in their development.

Statistics show the two primary reasons kids quit a sport is because parents pressure them to improve, or are over the top with their behavior as a spectator. It is very important not to minimize these stats, and at the same time recognize involving yourself in the right way is key to your child's success. Be sensitive to being overinvolved in things that are harmful.

It is so important to let the process take over. This requires parents to be patient. I had to learn this virtue because I wanted everything to be done yesterday, especially when recruiting. I will never forget when I first put my level of patience to a true test.

In 1989, we were recruiting this list of players who would make their decisions in the fall.

- Kenny Anderson (#1 player in America)
- Malcolm Mackey (McDonalds All American)
- Darryl Barnes (McDonalds All American)

- Ivano Newbill (#1 player in Georgia)
- Matt Geiger (transfer from Auburn)

Throughout the summer and into September I anxiously wanted to push the envelope and get some indication of where we stood with these players. Bobby Cremins would just say, "Kevin, it is a process. Be patient." If I allowed my impatience to go outside the process, I may have done something to negatively impact what we were hoping to accomplish. I finally calmed down, took his advice, and in November our successful recruiting class was rated the best in college.

Don't Allow a Parent's Wisdom to Backfire

I have been told many times in my career that I have a special gift for being able to empathize with kids of all ages. I can relate to what they are experiencing in the different stages of their lives on and off the court. I used this wisdom initially with college players in my coaching career. My coaching and player development activities after my college coaching career has given me the opportunity to also connect with kids as young as first grade.

Obviously being able to put myself mentally into all different scenarios comes from my experiences growing up. I am a sensitive person, so events in my life, good or bad, have left an impression. Some of my wisdom comes from growing up with nine brothers and sisters. I struggled academically in elementary school along with all the memories of not making grade school basketball teams.

There is one area I cannot relate to in youth sports today, and that is parent behavior. I am always worried about the impact of parent behavior when I train all the kids I work with. I cannot relate because I grew up in an era where parents encouraged kids to play sports but their presence at events was not part of their parenting. My mother never saw me play in high school or college. My dad maybe saw ten of my high school games. That's just the way it was back then. The players were left to deal with all situations faced when playing sports.

Parental involvement is the only part of training that bothers me because through experience I know if parents do not handle it right, it can only have a negative impact on your child's development. I try to explain to parents the role they need to play and how they can have a more positive impact on their kids. Honestly, much of the time what I am saying is just not being heard.

I don't know of any successful athlete making it because their parent controlled the path, but I do know of many who have wrecked the chances for their child to be successful. I also know generations of successful players who made it with very little or no parental involvement.

A parent's wisdom of knowing what it takes to be successful - in anything - can work against your child when assisting him in basketball. Try and think back when you were their age. Would you accept someone trying to force this basketball work ethic on you, especially when you could not relate to any of it?

Knowing what is needed for your child to reach his or her goal comes from your years of experience. Trying to put all of that knowledge at once into a mind that cannot relate to any of it will end up having the opposite effect. Mental maturity takes time. Kids below high school age just cannot comprehend the level of hard work required in committing to basketball.

I realized after a few years of training, as I saw parents pushing their kids to commit to working on their own, it was important to speak with them about what they were doing. My experience was telling me this behavior of working on their own happened around their sophomore year. Any parent pushing to do this before the player is ready will find it has a negative impact on the player's development.

I was speaking once to a large group of parents. I brought up the topic of expecting their child to get serious about spending more time improving on their own to practice the skills I was teaching. One parent, who happened to be a brain surgeon, spoke up and validated what I was saying. He said the brain is not capable of understanding that type of competitiveness at a young age. He confirmed that for most kids, this type of thinking can be more easily accepted starting at the ages of 14, 15 or 16.

This was great feedback. My knowledge came from my training experience with many players, but his knowledge of the maturing brain of a child provided the medical support I used often in my speeches and conversations with parents going forward.

As I continued to train players, I asked parents not to watch my training sessions with their kids. Many parent's behavior as they observed their child's practices focused on giving their kid instructions. I also watched these kids not having fun on many occasions while their parents were present during the workouts.

It was amazing to watch the kids having fun being kids and not having to look over their shoulder for acceptance from their parents on what they were doing during the workouts when the parents were not present for training sessions. Their skill development also progressed more quickly. Many parents would tell me it was great driving home because their child would be telling them what they did instead of their time together being about the parent critiquing their workout.

There is a fine line between enthusiastically encouraging your child and pushing them too hard. Guard against critiquing or pressuring them into reaching his goal. Positive, supportive feedback is critical. Negative feedback does not help.

Consider the following example when working to provide positive rather than negative feedback. Think about the situation where your child may not be taking shots when they are available to take them. It is obvious that he or she is afraid, so your input needs to be positive. A negative response would be, "If so and so is shooting, then you need to shoot. You are wide open. Shoot the ball." A positive response would be, "You have worked hard on your shooting and you have a nice shot. When you are open the next time, think about shooting."

The ideal response after watching your child play should be as simple as, "Good game, you're getting better … just keep working hard." This statement is encouraging and usually leads to your child critiquing their game play to you. Kids are very aware of their mistakes when competing and know where their skills are at in comparison to others.

Parenting and coaching are both teaching roles. Our priority is all about progress and this cannot be accomplished without motivation. This is a simple concept but sometimes hard to embrace. As I have listened to parents over the years, they all have good intentions. They believe they are correct in what they are saying to their kids but it is often so far off base due to of the lack of understanding of the learning process. It is all about encouragement. And if a parent needs help, there are parenting books explaining words that should and should not be used along with how to successfully watch your child's progress in addition to providing positive feedback.

What I don't understand is how parents will often act or say things differently when in a sports environment with their kids in comparison to other parenting situations they find themselves in. For the most part, a parent will know how to say the right things to build confidence in their child outside the sports environment, but will often say or do the exact opposite while their child is playing a sport.

Since parental involvement is an issue, I have tried to come up with analogies. Watching your child learn a sport is much harder than learning a subject in school. You can train your brain quicker to understand something new whereas teaching your body to do something new takes a lot longer. Another reason the process is slower is because the kids are trying to learn in public. This is intimidating and distracting for them.

The thing that stimulates parent's minds to get overly involved when watching their child in sports comes from comparing abilities with other kids, and seeing where their child needs improvement. The problem arises from parents instinctively wanting their kids to be just as good as, or better than others - in anything. This type of knowledge is the reason parents often become overbearing and push the process along faster, which is totally opposite the way professionals teach.

These same results would happen in the educational system if there were bleachers in the classroom so parents could be spectators. Imagine observing teachers and critiquing their methods of teaching along with comparing their child to others! Instead, parents have to wait for parent teacher meetings to receive progress reports and discuss methods of improving in any areas of concern.

Everyone learns at a different pace. Some kids are way ahead of others when playing sports as well as in the classroom. The problem happens when we try to make up the differences at a pace that is not healthy to the learning process. This is always happening in sports.

As a parent, when you see and feel that your child is lacking in areas while comparing them to other kids, this is the perfect time for words of encouragement. Tell them, "Everyone learns at a different pace, keep working hard." If possible, give examples about a classroom scenario where your child is superior.

I am an avid reader, and am always trying to learn better approaches to motivate a player to improve. Everything focuses on the right actions and the use of the right words. It takes years of experience through trial and error trying to teach the learning process faster. The hard part is that there is not one process for everyone. Everyone learns at a different pace. This subject is critical to a coach's success. It has to be at the forefront for all parents when your child is playing basketball.

Learning The Hard Lessons - Your Child Must Be Committed for THEIR OWN Reasons

Let your child take complete control of their commitment to becoming a good basketball player so they can establish and define their work ethic. Self-motivation builds confidence, and is a great asset which will be used long after their basketball playing days are over.

There is one thing I try to instill in the parents of players I train. Parents have to give their child credit that they know what they are doing wrong when they are playing. Also, your child realizes what he or she has to do to get better. Yet, parents believe giving this type of information is good parenting advice.

Parents must let their child learn to love the game by themselves. If they are playing the game because of you, it then becomes a job. Jobs last just so long. It is inevitable that this will not last long. When a person loves something they will keep going back to it, always asking questions and searching for better approaches with which to improve.

I have not come across many players in all my years of player development who "love the game." Most kids like to play, but are not willing to put in the time to love it. They need to respect the hard work that goes into becoming good. Without preparation they cannot expect success.

My work ethic began to take shape when I committed myself to becoming a college player. It continued in college with my goal of one day wanting to play in the NBA. My career has had many challenges and I have no doubt my strength to face those challenges comes from the hard lessons of learning that without hard work it is tough to succeed in anything.

After being in coaching for about seven years at the beginning of my career, I started to notice a comparison of our former players who were out in the business world and their work ethic while in college. It got to the point that I could predict the level of success our players would have when they got into the "real world."

I consider my own journey as an example. I learned on my own what was needed to find success in basketball. I worked hard at it and became very disciplined, setting up my own running program, running sprints every day in the New York heat. Those afternoon individual drill sessions in the park, and never letting up, taught me so much. It paid off in many ways, but the character trait I learned was to never give up.

Key to Remember

- Parents play a huge role in the development process of their child. Avoid the shortfalls that come with being a concerned parent and getting too involved. Learn to use your wisdom at the right time.
- It is important for parents to understand that a basketball environment is an incredible time in which to teach character building because competition presents so many opportunities. Don't use this time by being a typical spectator because, without realizing it, your child follows your example.
- The process of learning a school subject or a sport is very similar. Trying to constantly improve at either is a progression which needs a great deal of patience from parents. If parents try and speed up the process, they will frustrate their child. This will slow down improvement.

- A parent has two very important roles to play in order for your child to constantly improve and become the best he or she can become. First, remember your actions during the actual competition and your comments after the games. Your actions need to be taken seriously. They are being evaluated by your child and others. Second, know how to communicate to your child in a positive way after a game.
- If you cannot take care of these two things, you are hurting your child's chances of having success on his or her basketball journey.
- Your child's success hinges on you letting go when it comes to his or her individual improvement. Trust that your child understands what needs to be worked on. Stay away from negative comments because most of the time you are telling them something of which they already are aware.

CHAPTER 20

Beware of Negativity. Are You Part of the Problem or the Solution?

"God grant me the serenity to accept the things I cannot change,
Courage to change the things that I can,
And the wisdom to know the difference."
— THE SERENITY PRAYER

Teach the right life values through your own behavior. Teaching your child life lessons during their basketball journey will not be an easy task. Parents cannot just live in the moment as they experience their child's basketball participation journey. Parents always need to think of the big picture and the outcomes over the long term.

It will be a long process with many outside influences creating challenges. Always remember parents need to be supportive of other players, coaches and parents, but ultimately your child is the only person to be concerned about. Your child's behavior is strongly influenced by your words and actions.

It is important to understand how positive experiences can impact everything. It is not just about your child's basketball journey, but the life lessons foundation that is being put in place which will impact your child for the rest of their life.

A critical lesson for your child is to learn not to worry about things out of their control. These teaching opportunities come to light so many times when playing youth sports. I have listened to and watched what has become the norm, that parents support their child's frustrations after the games, blaming coaches, officials or teammates.

With so many games being played today we are creating a generation of kids who are making excuses for why their playing wasn't what it should have been. There is not any personal accountability. This is sending such a bad message. You and your child have no control over the actions, thoughts and decisions of coaches, officials or team-mates. What a great time to explain the Serenity Prayer: "God grant me the serenity to accept the things I cannot change, courage to change the things that I can, and the wisdom to know the difference."

As coaches and parents, it is our job to get the kids to not focus on excuses. We try to teach them the correct way to think in order to control what they can so that they can gain confidence. Confidence then leads to improvement.

Trying to avoid negativity through your child's journey to excel in basketball is going to be hard work. This will be even more so if they choose to play a full off-season game schedule to include Travel Team participation along with the in-season school team schedule. More competition brings more critiquing, not just of performances, but of all the fanfare surrounding games.

Always remember to guard against critiquing your child's performances. You will have every opportunity to be an over-invested spectator. Fight the urge. Leave that to other parents. There are so many responsibilities that a player has when playing. It is impossible to ever come close to playing a perfect, mistake-free game. Even Michael Jordan never played anywhere near a perfect game!

When training players over time, I listen and observe their parents at the workout sessions and pay attention to their responses to the games their child has played. I often try to coach the parents on the part they should be playing in order to steer away from critiquing their child's workouts and games.

It always surprises me when many parents who know what not to do just can't seem to avoid staying overly involved. Proper communication when encouraging and critiquing is all about the words, and how they are used.

There were two parents who were both very involved with each of their son's basketball success. Both players were college prospects and had just finished their high school junior season.

One parent handled things in a way that lead to the end of his son's ambition to play ball, but the other was able to support and, at the same time, get out of the way and enable his son to find his way and continue to play and excel at the college level. Both parents had the identical intentions, but their approaches made the difference in their child's basketball future.

Player #1 had been training for three years. During his junior season I contacted some Division I programs to evaluate his talent. I successfully got him on the radar of college coaches who had an interest in recruiting him.

His father was a great guy, but was always talking to his son about negative things he observed either at my training sessions or after the games. When colleges started contacting his son the dad became obsessed with wanting his son to get better quickly.

I had told this young man many times he had worked very hard to get to this point and at the same time there were things he needed to improve to get to the next level in order to be ready for the college coaches' evaluations. His dad took a different approach, which was less positive recognition and more emphasis on the weaknesses in his son's game and how critical it was to fix them quickly.

I was preparing to work with this player in the spring of his junior year and assisting him in his recruiting going forward, but he made the decision that he did not want to play basketball anymore. I was shocked. This young man was going to play Division I college basketball, but quit because of how his father was handling the situation.

Player #2 had been training for four years and was working very hard on getting college coaches to see him play. His dad had done a fabulous job teaching and working with his son to develop his skills to be in a position to play college basketball. I believed he was a legitimate college prospect.

I sat with the dad during many of his son's games. He was quiet during the games but talked to me about areas his son needed to improve to see if I agreed. His son was undersized at 5'10," but was an excellent shooter, one of the best I had seen and was playing on a sponsored Travel Team.

The summer between his junior and senior season was important for his participation on the sponsored Travel Team tournament circuit to make a good impression on Division I College coaches.

His dad informed me that his son had decided not to play Travel Ball anymore. He asked me to talk with his son. I talked through things with the son. I supported his decision because if he went ahead and played, most likely he would have played poorly because he didn't want to participate and would have ended up with him not impressing college coaches.

His dad struggled with his decision asking, "Now what do we do about college?" I said, "We go to plan B. Get coaches to see him play his senior season." His son went on and played Division I ball, becoming a starter his junior and senior year.

I tell you these two stories because both of these parents were heavily involved in their son's basketball careers. Player #2's father was much more involved than Player #1's father. The big difference was that their approaches were completely opposite.

Player #1's father communicated to his son all the things his son did or did not do, or what he should have done, acting as a coach and not as a parent. The father was always dissecting his son's practices or games. What the father did not realize was that his son knew exactly what he needed to work on, all along knowing what his mistakes were when playing. The father, when it was all over, was the reason his son did not succeed. The son did everything he was supposed to do for success. His father got in the way.

Player #2's father communicated with his son in a positive way, leading his conversations with compliments and getting him to work on his weaknesses. I never heard him dissect his son's performance after a game.

The moral of these two stories is for parents to monitor themselves and their behavior. Don't slow your child's development process down with negative behavior or comments.

Key to Remember:

- Being a parent is very challenging in general. Being a parent whose child is playing a team sport is even tougher because they are not only dealing with their child, but coaches, teammates and their parents.
- The team sport type of environment is set up for being judgmental. It can become very damaging to a child's success. A parent's mentality should be that of a "politician," watching what you say, staying on the fence and never hurting anyone's feelings.
- A parent needs to develop their own skills to assist in helping their child succeed. Understanding the right and wrong ways to communicate with their child and keeping a positive image with coaches are two parental skills that are needed in making this journey successful.

CHAPTER 21

Recipe for a Successful Life – Don't Miss Out by Being a Spectator

> *"What you are as a person is far more important than what you are as a basketball player."*
> – John Wooden

This chapter is focused on how youth sports provides many opportunities to teach the right values and life lessons to a child so they can be carried through the child's entire life.

Good coaches use their opportunities to teach life lessons to their players because of the situations presented through their basketball coaching roles. As a parent, you have the same opportunities within the sports environment. If you remain focused on your parenting role of teaching and mentoring your child as he or she is participating, you will be more effective in taking advantage of the many teaching moments you will have with your son or daughter.

Be On the Lookout for Life Lesson Teaching Moments

The phrase, "teaching life skills" is used constantly by college coaches in all sports when describing the most important aspects of what goes on inside their programs. I don't believe the average sports fan or parent understands what coaches are talking about when they hear this phrase.

Any college coach will tell you that their team is just an extension of their family. They are always concerned about the well-being of their players, and want the same outcome as a parent does with their child. Like a parent who is teaching their child to understand right and wrong behavior, coaches spend the majority of their time reinforcing these same life lessons.

I know from my own experience how a college coach can have a lifelong impact on a player's success by seizing the opportunity on and off the court to instill good character in all sorts of situations.

The formula for being a successful coach is complicated, but the most important ingredient is in treating players as people, not basketball players. As an example, if a player had a career-ending injury, a coach should not take away his scholarship because as a person, the player's education is far more important.

Coaches are always reinforcing the "off the court" behavior parents teach as their child grows up by monitoring their actions outside of basketball. These actions include such things as how important it is to be on time, doing homework, completing assignments and being polite to others.

The "on court" behavior provides coaches many opportunities to teach life skills when competition brings out the player's emotions. Players must have the right mindset when confronted with positive or negative moments while competing, which is something that happens in every basketball program. A player has negative thoughts about where he or she stands on the team because of decisions made by coaches. A coach cannot leave this up to the player to figure out on their own. As long as the player has negative thoughts, their progress to improve will stall. Individual meetings have to take place until they understand.

The countless opportunities during competition gives coaches a chance to teach a strong character foundation through the many examples on how to act. It is a player's internship for learning how to handle the ups and downs of life.

Your child playing basketball gives you the same opportunities a coach has of building a good character foundation. The majority of kids will not have the luxury of a college coach teaching them important life lessons, so by not taking the time now, you are missing a great parenting opportunity.

A child's participation in sports needs to be taken seriously so parents can anticipate the life lesson opportunities they will have to teach. Your mental approach has to be all about teaching when your child's feelings are being challenged.

I will always remember a trip I took to Texas to evaluate a point guard. We were desperately needing to sign a top notch guard and it was getting late into the high school season, so time was running out on evaluations. I carefully watched the player in warm-ups and was impressed. The game started and I became really impressed with his knowledge, shooting skills and defense. I felt that I had found our guy.

What happened next was startling. By the middle of the second quarter his team was down 20 points and this player turned into a raving maniac. I was hoping at half time his coach or someone would get him under control, but things stayed the same when the second half started. I left the game really disappointed because his basketball skills were worthy of a scholarship to Georgia Tech. His people skills were not.

Following are some different scenarios that are just a few examples of how the competitive part of a child's "on court" actions can be rewarding for both of you. Compare these basketball participation situations to later life situations.

1. Trying out to make the team – applying for a job.
2. Competing against your teammates for playing time – getting a promotion at work.
3. Competing in public against opponents is similar to becoming a successful employee.

Those three situations can be used to come up with so many lessons that need to be taught in order to have a successful working career. These scenarios, if not taught correctly, can mold a person's character the wrong way. The wrong way can lead to making excuses, becoming judgmental, blaming others for lack of success which reduces the chances to reach full potential.

I realized not too long into my coaching career that to be successful, worrying about players on an individual basis was more important than what offense and defense I should run.

I had the pleasure of sitting next to Bobby Cremins for 20 seasons and I can say beyond any doubt he received the respect and trust of his players. All of this respect and trust was due to the time and effort he put into player relationships OFF the court, always worrying about and managing the well-being of each and every player.

The formula for being a successful coach is complicated. The biggest obstacle to success is getting the trust of the players, with the reward being lifelong thanks. Gaining a player's trust is crucial, so all communication will get full attention. Gaining this trust does not happen overnight. Players need confirmation as they go through different experiences on and off the court. They need to see consistent honesty in all communication.

Creating a bond with a player is the most difficult aspect of coaching. The most important method to teaching is being able to give constructive criticism, but a player who has not grown to trust takes what is being said as just criticism.

Head coaches use different strategies to attain this trust as quickly as possible, using assistants to reinforce their message, sometimes playing the role of "good cop, bad cop." The best help comes from players who already believe in the program.

Watching players gain trust is very rewarding because at that point coaches know their wisdom is being passed on. The most enjoyable part of coaching is having former players staying in touch and always thanking you for what you taught them about life. It is never about basketball philosophy. This type of recognition comes my way often, and it is so rewarding to know I made an impression on a person's life.

A coach's biggest obstacle does not come into play for parents. The trust is already there for parents, so why not use youth basketball experiences as parenting opportunities to build a foundation for your child's life skills? The reward for this type of parenting is respect for life.

I believe parents lose an incredible opportunity in character building with their kids. They get caught up in the drama of the competition. They often watch games as a typical fan or spectator. They miss teaching examples everywhere that can benefit their child.

But the opportunities to build character are limitless. Every time your child competes you are given many chances to talk later about her or his behavior. The examples are priceless because they are happening in public.

We all learn by example. The more examples, the quicker the learning process. Use this basketball journey to mold their character. Parents watching their child compete will reveal their character first as they react to different situations. This is their time to work at making the old saying about sports come to life: "sports builds character."

As you know, being a parent is very complicated, always teaching and being focused on a child's mental growth as they try to build character. Their character will be with them forever so understanding how parents can accomplish this during their basketball journey is a key part of the extension of their parental role.

How Do We React When We Don't Get What We Want?

One of many similarities between life and playing a sport is striving for something that is important to us. We are so often focused on a goal. There is always something we want. The destination can be such an emphasis.

There comes a time in life when we recognize it is more about the journey than the destination. Throughout our lives we may be fortunate to reach our goals, our destinations, but we come to learn that life is so much more about the journey. There are times we get what we want. But the journey is often so much more about how we cope and behave when we don't get what we want.

When we are a spectator watching a game, we are so focused on winning and losing, so focused on the goal of excelling. Results are what it is all about. This is what drives the exhilaration and fun of sports.

It is so important that parents bring their wisdom of life with them when engaging with their child as they participate in the sport of basketball, or any sport for that matter. Don't get caught up in being a spectator.

If a child chooses to play an individual sport, a parent's focus during competition would be totally different watching only their child's performance. It should not change when they are playing a team game. But because we put so much emphasis on the end result, we get caught up critiquing their teammates. By doing this, parents are splitting valuable time watching their child and being concerned about the other players.

Anyone who plays a sport will strive for some goal for themselves or their team. But on their journey, they will most likely face a great deal of adversity. How they react when they don't get what they want will be where the real story is told. This is what creates all the teaching moments throughout the youth sports environment.

The foundation for teaching is all centered on how to deal with ups and downs, winning and losing, positive and negative, good and bad and not getting what you want and how to cope with things that don't go our way. These are emotions we all go through in life.

A child will experience so many challenges on and off the court during their character molding years while playing basketball. For those parents who are not getting caught up in the game as a fan and spectator, there are many opportunities to teach the right behaviors that will help them throughout their life beyond their days of playing the game of basketball.

Being a coach has taught me how to be a better parent. Being a parent taught me how to be a better coach. I learned as a coach that emotions surrounding "success" have to be managed. When experiencing success, there can be a tendency to let up. This leads to failure. A sport, like life, is an emotional roller coaster.

To be able to use a child's basketball experience as a life lesson teaching tool, parents have to be disciplined, always remembering that they can't get caught up in the emotions or take it personally when a decision is made by a coach or teammate that negatively impacts their child.

My wife and I have used the participation in sports for our kids to mold their character in so many ways. I chose an intense and time-consuming profession when becoming a college coach. It often kept me away from home. At times it was tough on my wife and two children. My kids were three years apart. I have a daughter and son who were both involved in sports.

My wife was like any other person who followed sports. She assumed a college coach's job was all centered on teaching the sport so the players would continue to improve. This assumption changed one time when she said that I had finally brought my job home.

The first time she began to realize my coaching duties went way beyond what she expected was when our kids began playing sports. My son was 7 years old and playing in his first recreation basketball league. Because of my job commitments, I had missed his first three games. He was excited that I was finally going to see him play.

I listened to my wife scream instructions to my son. Things like, "rebound," or, "play defense." She sounded no different than all of the other parents watching the game. I softly said, "don't do that." I briefly explained why. "He recognizes your voice over the others screaming and the commands are not realistic for him to respond to at this time."

She first thought she had to just sit and watch without saying anything. I told her to go ahead and yell, but be positive and enthusiastic about what he is doing, not what he should be doing. I told her to just change what she was saying somewhat to positive phrases such as, "good hustle, nice pass, good job."

My wife gave me another opportunity after the game to support her with a problem concerning our son's playing time. A rule of the league was that every kid was to play at least an entire half. She said he had not played a whole half yet. She was going to talk to the coach.

After the game my son came running over to me, excited because I was there. He was describing things he did during the game. My wife mentioned again she was going to talk to the coach. I asked her to look at our son. He was so excited. He did not play a full half in this game, but it was not bothering him. Kids are uncomfortable when their parents get involved with their coaches. And what is most important is that when it starts to bother him, it is then his responsibility to talk to his coach.

This game was the beginning of my wife understanding that my job went way beyond skills teaching. Later I explained in more detail what we had discussed at the game. I knew our son recognized her voice because of my own experience coaching in a loud environment.

Players I coached would tell me they could hear my instructions over incredible noise during games. As a young coach, I would yell commands to my players while they were playing. They would later tell me it was distracting and upsetting because publicly I was verbally telling everyone what they should be doing. I was, in essence, throwing them under the bus.

My professional experience dealing with the feelings and the mindset of players on the college level was identical to coaching my kids through their highs and lows of playing a sport. It is all relevant. No matter what the age of the players, feelings are feelings.

Another example of how the environment of a sport impacts kid's behavior is when my son was a Georgia Tech ball boy. While working every home game, he listened to Coach Bobby Cremins' pre-game, half time, and post-game talks to the team. My wife and I realized the valuable lessons he was being taught. I can honestly say there is no course my son ever took in school (and he has two masters degrees), that has taught him what he learned just by listening to what Bobby would tell our players.

When my son was eleven we were driving home after a game we had just won. Out of nowhere my son proceeded to tell me we might have chemistry problems on the team. He said one of our players does not get along with a couple of his team-mates. This knowledge came from him being in the locker room, listening to conversations. First of all, I was amazed that at his age he understood how important team chemistry was. I also took his information seriously and kept an eye on the situation so that this player's feelings did not affect our teams' play.

Bobby Cremins' pre-game messages were focused on the game plan and player assignments and roles. Half time was about adjustments with X's and 0's, but even more so about individual player and team emotions. Post-game was all about attitude, how to act and what to say to friends, family and the media regardless of whether we won or lost.

An example on how to deal with emotions after an unbelievable win was when we had beaten North Carolina with a shot at the buzzer at home. It was a big upset. Bobby's post game talk was going over how to act after an emotional win. He told the players to say, "We were lucky," and reminding them how we felt after losing in familiar fashion. It was all about being humble.

My kids went on to play sports in high school and college. My daughter was a swimmer/crew and my son played basketball. Both my kids were well-grounded be-cause of their sports journey. As a parent I was able to find opportunities for life lesson teaching moments addressing their emotions as they experienced the ups and downs of participation in their sports.

To this day my wife talks about how I handled the drama of our kid's sports experiences, always talking with them about their behavior and molding their characters. They were reminded about the challenges they were facing and that how they responded was defining who they would become for the rest of their lives.

Highest player performance and winning has become the primary goal for those playing youth sports. I am in no way saying this is not a worthy focus. Your child won't succeed at making the next level teams on his journey to one day playing college basketball if not for the emphasis on highest player performance. I believe, though, that it doesn't have to be one or the other when it comes to excelling or learning life lessons. It can be both.

We all know as parents, there is no higher priority than dealing with our kids and their emotional growth and well-being. The time your child spends participating in their sport is truly a great opportunity for you to coach and mentor things far more important than winning and losing. Don't get caught up being a spectator and miss the chances for more teaching moments to enhance the character building opportunities presented by youth sports. After all, isn't that the original intention for youth sports?

Key to Remember

- College coaches are an extension of their player's parents, always teaching life skills and preparing them for the next stage in life. Coaches spend very little time with players talking about basketball outside of practice. There is a lot of ingredients that go into being a successful coach, and most of what is needed is not basketball-related.
- The biggest ingredient is having an individual relationship with the players, caring about their lives as people, not just basketball players. It's about taking opportunities to ask how their families and friends are doing, talking about classes, just staying connected to each and every player.
- The parenting is done by teaching character, using any opportunity as a lesson needing to be taught on or off the court. There are so many of these lessons off the court. For instance, the importance of not being late. Players are taught they should always be on time because it is disrespectful to have someone wait for them. On the court is where players can find so many issues that need attention such as how to act after losing, or when a player doesn't understand their role.

- Take time spent as a spectator and turn it into parenting time. Use all of the opportunities that occur when playing a sport to teach your child the correct way to handle the different issues.

CHAPTER 22

The Competitive Journey for Your Child — Create The Plan

"Practice does not make perfect. Only perfect practice makes perfect."
— Vince Lombardi

P arents have a big role to play in their child's youth basketball journey. By reading this book you are now so much more aware of the misconceptions and challenges in youth basketball in America. It also enables you to be able to explain to your child why they need to be doing things a little different than most.

On their own, no child would ever think about going in another direction. A parent's guidance is critical to doing the right things and making adjustments to steer away from anything not in their best interests.

Webster's definition of "process" is a continuing development involving many changes, a particular method of doing something with all the steps involved. This is easy to understand, but extremely difficult when trying to stay the course.

It does not matter what level of basketball your child is playing. Begin this process of development, their journey, by putting together a plan that gives them every chance of fulfilling a dream. Each stage of your child's journey has a dream level. Their hopes as early as elementary school are to make their school team. Throughout every stage your child also has a dream level for excelling. Excelling is so often measured by the accomplishment of becoming a starter on the team.

There are five sections for consideration in any plan you create for your child. I have listed them in the right sequence. I recommend not changing the sequence as you create your plan.

1. Find a Skills Instructor

   The first section of the process is so important. Finding an instructor to properly teach your child footwork, how to shoot and dribble is your first order of business. Start early, but know that it is never too late to get started to correctly change these skills.

   Having all the knowledge I have shared with you in this book and believing your child will take the road less traveled will not work without them being ready to learn and work at building the correct skills. The right instructor in your local community should be part of your team of resources to support your child throughout his or her basketball journey.

2. Individual Skill Development

   Have a plan for your child's individual skill development. Your child must make personal skill development his or her priority. Remember that on all levels, when it is time to be evaluated to make a team or be chosen to be a starter, it will be all centered on a player's personal talent.

   Personal basketball growth only happens if there is significant improvement of individual skills as players work thru their plan. As their legs and body strength develops over the years with consistent skill training, their improvement will continue to give them opportunities to excel and play a meaningful team role or reach that dream of becoming a starter.

   This type of commitment is extremely difficult, but the journey is so rewarding. The work ethic your child will develop through their commitment to becoming the "best they can be" will create habits they will apply in every area of their life going forward beyond basketball.

   Your child will be establishing confidence during this process, which in turn will make playing the game so much easier. The next phase to becoming a good player is learning how to play the team game and that can only be accomplished when their minds are free of worrying about personal weaknesses.

   During games your child will begin to feel comfortable, which leads to better listening and understanding, thus ensuring an awareness of so many more aspects of the game that are needed to continue to play beyond high school. This puts your child in total control of his or her future.

   During my years as a college coach I witnessed many of our players who realized their weaknesses when they were hit head on in their freshman season, often because of deficiencies with proper technique and individual skill development levels. In this regard, one player I coached at Georgia Tech comes to mind. This player was not heavily recruited out of high school. He didn't play in the Travel Ball system, and no other major college recruited him. He was 6' 5" and played inside in high school. Many did not think he could make the transition to become a perimeter college player because he was not a good shooter. He had poor shooting form and lacked dribbling skills.

His first objective as a freshman was to learn how to shoot correctly. He chose Mark Price to train him. Mark was a former Georgia Tech All American, who at 5'11" is still considered one of the best shooters to ever play in the NBA. Mark has also become exceptional at developing player skills. He is now a head coach at the college level.

This player's transformation in becoming a perimeter player did not take long because of a work ethic that was amazing. To this day I can't say I have ever witnessed anything like it. I can't imagine any successful athlete working any harder than this player.

His shooting and ball handling skills continued to get better each year, and midway through his junior season it was evident that his mission was to play in the NBA. This was inconceivable when thinking about his level of skill when he began his college career. His incredible mental toughness and drive was now making this dream a reality.

The player was Matt Harpring. He went on to have a stellar career in the NBA. He played most of his career with the Utah Jazz.

A moment I will never forget was when Matt played his final college game. It was in the ACC tournament at Greensboro Coliseum in North Carolina. With a few minutes remaining in the game, we took him out and 25,000 fans gave him a standing ovation for three minutes. This was amazing in and of itself, but even more so because the majority of fans in attendance were not Georgia Tech fans.

Their appreciation came from watching Matt throughout his college career. He was not a gifted basketball athlete, but he worked so hard to develop into a first round NBA draft choice. They had no idea how hard he worked behind the scenes as his dream transitioned into reality and a personal miracle.

3. Charting Game Performances

I have attended an incredible number of games over my 35 years on my own basketball journey. I've sat in bleachers around parents witnessing all types of behavior. The one consistency has been parents cheer for their child but for the most part they were fans getting caught up in the drama of the game, which is normal behavior.

On the other hand, I would be observing the same games differently. I watched games as a quiet spectator. I always focused on the player, observing shot selection, defensive containment, assists, turnovers, always keeping an eye on their personal behavior.

Use your child's games as a learning tool. Chart only his or her performance, not team statistics. Personal charting is identifying how, where and why things happened or not. Here are a few considerations when developing your plan for charting performance:

- Location on the floor from which your child is scoring?
- Location on the floor from which your child is struggling to score?
- How is he or she committing turnovers?
- How is he or she making assists?
- Successful or unsuccessful containment on defense?
- Toughness going after the ball on rebounds
- Forgot about rebounding both offensively and defensively?
- How many times, if any, did they make an offensive move using their weak hand?

These game summaries will show your child's strengths and weaknesses at their present stage of development. Charting how many times they go to get a rebound – not getting the rebound, but putting themselves in the position to get one. Chart how many non-effective dribbles he or she is using. These are just a couple of examples.

This kind of information will help reinforce some of the key points a good instructor will be teaching your child in developing their skills for becoming a better player.

Charting will also remove a parent from some of the emotional game drama because if their child is in the game, they cannot take their eye off of him or her due to what they are charting.

Kids today do not understand their roles because of the sheer quantity of games they play. They have little interest, time or concern with final team game stats. The majority of kids today feel they can fit the role of a shooter AND a scorer because they have been able to make a couple of shots using both roles.

Recently a friend of mine asked if I would watch his child play and give him any input that could assist his son in playing better. He was 6" 6' and played inside. He was a strong kid. He said he didn't score much because other players were taking the shots, and very seldom passing inside.

After watching him play, it was very obvious to me ways he could score and make an impact on his team while giving him his own identity. My evaluation: he received the ball twice inside against a zone. Both times he put the ball on the floor and forced a shot with two players on him. He missed both shots but followed them up getting two offensive rebounds and 4 points.

I met with him after the game and told him he does not fit the description of a scorer or shooter but could become a heck of a rebounder on both sides of the ball. I told him his points will come from offensive rebounds, put backs and foul shots. I said to be relentless going to the boards because college coaches are always looking for that type of player. He took my advice went on to receive a scholarship to a NCAA Division II college.

The game summary you can create is identical to how a college coach provides proof to players when communicating their role to them. Roles can change, but that change is always left up to the individual player improving on weaknesses.

This method of analyzing your child's performances should be used when they are playing Travel Ball or school team games. It is also important for you not to get involved in critiquing your child about what you charted.

Let your child study his or her own performance. Share the summary with their skill development instructor to take into account when setting training objectives together. This is the way your child will then identify what type of player he or she is. It will begin to teach your child all the parts of the game that are meaningful.

4. Leverage Travel Ball Season for Your Child

Our entire youth basketball system overemphasizes playing as many games as possible as a primary plan of attack for player development. Now that you have the knowledge shared in this book, don't ignore the fact your child cannot improve skills by playing more games.

Playing for a Travel Team is a key part of the US youth basketball system. It can be a positive experience for your child. I find it is often not a good experience for players and parents because they have the wrong expectations of what their participation should provide them.

Your child's participation in Travel Ball will increase their focus and time commitment for playing games. They may enjoy participation, but don't expect it to develop individual basketball skills. And don't assume participation will automatically get him or her on a coach's radar and evaluated to play college basketball. The college coach evaluation process has to have its own specialized plan of attack.

As your child develops their plan for improving as an individual player, there are tradeoffs they will need to make, knowing they also have other priorities in life that are outside of basketball. They will have to manage their time available for academics, family, friends, team practices and playing games. There is only so much time in a day, week or month to do everything.

Decisions need to be made about how best to allocate time to the highest impact areas of basketball that will help your child improve. Knowing playing as many games as possible is not the formula for getting better, be sure to use any time playing Travel Ball to your child's advantage. Use their Travel Ball season to work on things that will test how well they are applying the things they are learning individually in game situations.

Three individual skills need constant attention: footwork, dribbling and shooting. One area when working on dribbling is to develop the weakest hand. Begin to use it as much as possible to build confidence. Shooting can be done with the same intention. Use the weak hand to shoot when the opportunity presents itself. As an example, when taking a layup or when getting an offensive rebound, use the offhand to put the ball back up.

Not many kids today use their weak hand because it takes a great deal of practice to get enough confidence to use it when playing. But when I do find one practicing this, they stand out. I immediately begin to watch this player with interest because I know he or she has put hard work into their weaknesses. Now I want to see other aspects of their game that sets them apart from others.

When planning my training sessions, I will always have what I call "offhand days."

In those sessions, which last 75 minutes, everything is done with the weak hand. The penalty for touching anything with their strong hand is three pushups.

I recently watched a middle school game and this one player took a left and right handed layup. They were so identical I could not tell if he was right or left handed. I was watching for clues to get my answer, hoping he would take a jump shot or foul shot. My question was answered watching him warm-up at half time.

If your child chooses to participate in Travel Ball, consider waiting until they have been taught individual skills correctly. Regardless of when they make the decision to participate, try not to play a full schedule because it leaves very little time to work on individual skill development.

It is discouraging working with kids trying to correct their shooting technique who play a full Travel Team schedule. We might train twice a week but that three or four game schedule on the weekend puts them right back into their original bad habits. They might only take a few shots in a game but think about all the shots taken in warm-ups and halftime.

If your child has worked hard at everything in the first four parts of the plan, the foundation will be in place for the final part which is getting evaluated by a college coach to play college basketball. I will devote the next chapter to this topic.

Key to Remember

- This chapter tells why you as a parent are so important to your child's basketball journey. Understanding this will be a process. There are a number of important parts that need to be addressed. Locating the right instructor to deal with fundamentals will be your first responsibility.

- It is so important to follow the details on how to improve your child's performance. The performance game plan will not work unless footwork and the proper way to shoot and dribble is taught. These fundamentals are linked in so many ways to other aspects of the game that it is vital they are taught correctly.

- Individual skill development is key to becoming a successful player. The majority of the time has to be put into personally getting better and improving on weaknesses by spending quality time with individual development.

- Use the Travel Ball system to your child's advantage. Turn it into quality time. Start charting information during the games so your child can benefit. Chart things such as focusing on where the shots are coming from, going to the basket to rebound, containing on defense and wasted dribbles. These are not typical basketball statistics, but are critical aspects of the game which need to be emphasized more seriously.

- If your child has college potential, you will have to create a plan to get the attention of college coaches.

CHAPTER 23

Knowledge is Power - Planning to Get the Attention of a College Coach

"To know is to know that you know nothing.
That is the meaning of true knowledge."
– SOCRATES

I f your child is playing high school basketball and has the dream of playing college basketball, this chapter is a must read. The path I am guiding players to take is less traveled by others in youth sports, but understanding how to navigate this journey gives your child an advantage most others will never get.

Your child's entire journey is based on your newfound understanding of how college coaches go about their business when recruiting. So make this paramount in your thinking. I recruited for 28 years and know exactly how coaches think, what they are looking for, and how they go about filling roster spots.

What frustrates me is watching families so engrossed in a youth sport with the hope of finding the edge for highest performance and getting evaluated for the chance to play college basketball, but because of their lack of knowledge I know it will most likely end in disappointment.

This is the stage where your knowledge becomes so powerful, putting you in full control because the odds your child faces trying to fill one of the 4000 college basketball roster spots will be difficult. But, by being in full control and focusing on the right things at the right times, his or her odds will be so much better!

There are different scenarios on how you can get the attention of college coaches, but remember your child's skills are the initial selling point to college coaches. You cannot be in a rush to get your child evaluated. Be patient because you have to wait until your child is basketball ready.

In the 90's Georgia Tech was one of the top basketball programs in the country. It was all due to the success we had recruiting. I was labeled by the national media as one of the best recruiters in all of college basketball. To me that meant I was a good salesman. I understood so much about the parents and players I was recruiting; thus I was selling the whole Georgia Tech basketball program. But I had to connect with parents and players by positioning the pieces that made up our program which were important to them.

There are many key things that go into any kind of a successful sale, but it cannot happen unless the salesperson "knows the product" and has the confidence it's being sold to the "right audience." The consideration must be made that a player is the product in this analogy and parents are selling to their target customer, the college coach.

Understanding what needs to be done to give parents a chance of making a sale to a college coach will keep them grounded when trying to get their child on a coach's radar. Knowing what pieces are important to the coach and how to go about molding and positioning their child so they fit the coach's needs is critical to a successful sale.

Parents should understand who they are "selling." Their child must be positioned properly to get on the coach's radar for evaluation. Then all the pieces about their child must fit what is important in the coach's criteria for what he needs to fill his open roster spot.

I see parents and players all the time randomly choosing a college program to send out personal information and videos just because there is something they like about the school. There is so much time and effort being wasted because there is a lack of understanding about who their right audience is, which – and how – college coaches and programs are each making their recruiting decisions, and what roster needs have to be addressed.

Understanding the Disparities Amongst the College Levels

This outline will give you a better understanding about the different levels of college basketball which will help you as you take into consideration your plan for getting the attention of college coaches for your child.

As you review the following outline, "Full Basketball Scholarship" implies all of the money is coming from the athletic department. The scholarship covers housing, tuition and books. "Partial Basketball Scholarship" implies the athletic department will supplement a portion of the cost and use financial assistance from other resources such as academic aid, government and student loans to lower your college coast.

The below "Available Rosters Spot" calculations were made assuming an average of three open spots annually for each basketball program.

1. NCAA Division I
   Number of Programs - men 351, women 349
   Available Roster Spots - men 1053, women 1047
   Recruiting Sources - high school, prep school (men only), junior college, international players
   Full Scholarships - men 13, women 15.

2. NCAA Division II
   Number of Programs - men 308, women 307
   Available Roster Spots - men 924, women 921
   Recruiting Sources - high school, prep school (men only), junior college, international players
   Partial Scholarships - men 10, women 10

3. NCAA Division III
   Number of Programs - men 421, women 442
   Available Roster Spots – men 1263, women 1326
   Recruiting Sources - high School, prep school (men only), international players
   Scholarships – there are no basketball program scholarships. Student athletes are eligible for academic aid, student loans and government loans.

4. NAIA Division I
   Number of Programs - men 105, women 105
   Available Roster Spots - men 315, women 315.
   Recruiting Sources - high school, prep school (men only), junior college, international players
   Partial Scholarships - men 11, women 11

5. NAIA Division II
   Number of Programs - men 125, women 124
   Available Roster Spots - men 375, women 372.
   Recruiting Sources - high school, prep school (men only), junior college, international players
   Partial Scholarships - men 6, women 6

When working to get on the coach's radar, here is a plan outline to facilitate your thinking. Use it to develop and implement your strategy to position your child with the right college coaches.

Step 1 – Your Child's List of Potential Colleges

Always start with a wide range of schools, and then narrow it down as you move along in the process.

I recommend exploring at least ten schools and basketball programs on the different levels.

1. *Personal Characteristics Wanted in a College*

   Parents need to make sure when choosing a college that it initially fits your child's needs outside of playing basketball. The first thing I ask players is, "If you never play basketball again what type of school would you like to attend?"

   Considerations need to include such things as academic requirements, enrollment size and location.

2. *Deciding on College Level to Match Your Child's Skill Level*

   This is crucial because as a parent you want to be communicating to the colleges that are on a level matching the level your child can successfully compete. This will ensure your child is a viable candidate for coaches to recruit.

   The earlier you can decide on this during your child's high school years, the better their chances are in connecting with coaches. Best to make this decision after high school freshmen year to begin investigating schools aside from NCAA Division I. The biggest mistake made by players and parents is just sitting back hoping and waiting for the Division I school to come calling.

   This does not mean you are giving up on Division I programs. It is just that your backup plan is going to require strategic planning. What you don't want to do is waste valuable time hoping for something that might not be attainable.

   All levels of college basketball have talented players and are extremely competitive. The NCAA Division III separates itself because of their strict academic admissions policies.

3. *Identify Position Needs for Each College*

   Finding colleges interested in your child's position is a smart sales move. This enables you to alert the right coaches who have a real need for what your child can offer.

These coaches will be your target audience, so investigating their needs has to be thorough. Just reviewing the college team's roster, identifying players in this position and their class year might not give you the full picture.

Spend time on the website reading articles about the team, media coverage after games, anything which will give the full story. Just reading rosters does not tell if they are redshirting a player or if there is the possibility that a player is no longer with the team.

This type of investigating really gives an insight into how coaches think and the words they use when describing different positions, which can be used when "selling" your child.

As an example, two colleges need a point guard, but one coach likes his point guards to be tall. The other prefers a player who is small, fast and quick. This knowledge will not only give a good indication if his position will be recruited, but the description of the kind of player they want. It will also be an attention getter when they look at your child's information.

Step 2 – Reaching Out to College Coaches

1. *The Information Package*
    Preparing this packet is an important part of the way you will initially communicate with coaches.
    - Cover letter. An introduction telling about who the player is and their interest in the school being applied to, both academically and basketball.
    - Basketball information. Players need to list their size, weight and position because it immediately tells the coaches if the player fits their needs. List the player's accomplishments and attach a schedule identifying them.
    - Academic information. GPA, SAT/ACT scores along with any awards and accomplishments.
    - Personal and school contacts. This information is just to make it readily available for the coaches.
    - Short video. Piece together game footage showing different aspects of your child's play dealing with their position. Do NOT send a highlight video. Coaches don't make final decisions based on a video, but they do decide after watching if they want to follow up. Coaches want to see your child's game against tough opponents. The more athletic the

opponent, the better opportunity your child will have of getting a follow-up interview.

2. *Timing for Reaching Out to College Coaches*

You can begin the process of getting to know the schools and programs at any time. The earlier the better. You want to express your feelings about the school and program but don't begin to sell your child's basketball ability too early.

Timing is a critical part of the process. There are small windows of opportunity to get a coach's attention. Coaches are on an internal yearly clock. This internal clock includes practice, season, recruiting, camps and vacation. They are programed to think with tunnel vision.

Patience is so important because we all tend to think we are going to miss out if we don't do things immediately. Remember, it is a process. And timing is everything!

I have personally assisted many parents in this process who totally trusted me training their children, but were always concerned about my suggestions as to when to send out information to colleges. I would remind them that above all, their child had to be ready to be evaluated. The more we trained together, along with their own development program, the better their chances would be.

When I am advising players who have college talent below Division I but have not been evaluated, I always wait until a player's senior season in late November to contact schools. This is because the early recruiting signing period is over. The college coaches that were not successful getting a roster spot filled are now looking for more players to evaluate.

This timing is always successful because I know how the college coach's recruiting world evolves. A parent cannot minimize making sure their child is basketball ready to get evaluated.

Step 3 - Proactive Ways to Get a College Coach's Attention

I have already mentioned that college coaches use Travel Ball as their main recruiting source for high school players. They work off sponsored team rosters. This is why if you are not playing on a sponsored team, you need to work on other approaches to be seen by college coaches.

Too many players go unrecruited because they don't realize there are other ways to get the attention of college coaches.

1. Marketing Yourself

    You should start contacting coaches as soon as you complete your freshman season. Send them your packet of information, but not the video. Coaches usually respond by sending a questionnaire. Know that their level of interest probably won't start until after your junior year. Make sure you continue to stay in contact with updates on how you are progressing, and always mentioning your desire to go to their school. Your initial correspondence needs to be addressed to the head coach but your follow-up information needs to go to an assistant. This will be the person you will communicate with. This is the coach who will eventually see your child play first.

    ▪ *College Summer Camp*

    Going to their camps is the best way to start a personal relationship with the coaches. Returning to their camp every summer is a great way to show your skill improvement.

    ▪ *Attend Games*

    Always make sure a coach knows you are in attendance. The best time to do this is about 30 minutes before the game during warm-ups. A simple hello and wishing them "good luck" is all you need to say. If you wait until the game is over, coaches are in a different frame of mind. Win or lose it is hard to get their attention.

    ▪ *Campus Visits*

    Whenever you visit a campus always schedule it around the coach's availability. You can set this up with an assistant, but hopefully you can talk with the head coach. Never feel uncomfortable because this happens often.

    ▪ *Network of College Coach Relationships*

    The best way to get the attention of a college coach is to find someone who has college coach contacts. This person could be a high school coach, former college coach, relative, neighbor, professor at the college or a friend of a friend. Every contact helps.

    You want to immediately make this school one of your choices if it meets all of your criteria. It is also very important that this contact has a relationship of respect because coaches get referrals all the time, but they do not spend time investigating unless they truly trust the person's opinion.

    My personal story is a good example for working to get kids on a college coach's radar. During the process of training, I make commitments to certain parents and players. I tell them I am willing to contact coaches "at the right time" to evaluate their talent.

I never have a problem worrying about living up to my promise that I will make the right connection with the right college coach because of my relationships with college coaches throughout the country. College coaches are confident that I know if a player can play for them because I have recruited players myself as a former college coach. If I say they should take a look at someone, they will take the time to see for themselves.

- Before contacting a coach, I will determine what college level a player is capable of competing.
- I will do my homework on what positions the coaches need to fill their roster. They trust I won't waste their time about a player.

Key to Remember

- The colleges you will be contacting do not recruit underclassman. Sending information during a player's junior year probably will go unnoticed. Sending it early is bad timing because coaches are completely focused on recruiting high school seniors.
- The earliest that packets should be mailed is June, right after your child's junior year. It is important to realize these coaches will be recruiting high school seniors for the next 10 months.
- There is nothing wrong with identifying a new college during senior year. College basketball programs recruit deep into the academic year, sometimes not finishing until June or July.
- Visiting campuses should begin after you choose the programs that interest you. Meet the coaching staff on these visits. Remember, if it is too early to pitch your basketball talent, just make it a friendly introductory visit.
- Visit campuses to get the coaches' attention. This needs to be scheduled around the head coach being available to meet you. The earliest this type of visit should happen is the summer before the senior year. This is when you deliver the packet of information. Because the coach is needing to know a player's position, you will have his attention.

- If the plan for your child to become the best they can become is followed, they will have the opportunity to create a plan on how to get evaluated by a college coach.
- Tactical decisions have to be made now and the initial part of this plan is to decide what level of college your child's talent best fits. This is important because parents need to be contacting colleges that will be interested. After deciding on the level of play your child is capable of playing at, parents then need to find the schools that are interested in recruiting the position their child plays.
- Parents have to strategically use methods to get the attention of college coaches which will lead to an evaluation.
- Always check with the high school counselor to ensure all core courses have been taken.
- Complete your due diligence on your targeted colleges or universities.

Be sure to access bonus content as my gift to you

www.KevinCantwellBasketball.com/p/gifts

WHY - The Reason for Writing This Book

You now have all my knowledge and experience from 40 years of coaching along with my own experiences playing basketball in high school and college. You have the blueprint you can use to help your child have a positive experience while playing youth basketball. You have everything you need to know about what it takes to make the team at every level and ultimately reach for the dream of one day playing college basketball.

Now that you have the formula and the step-by-step methodology, you may be asking yourself why I wrote this book. You might be wondering why I would give away what has taken me years to learn and develop in the pages of a book like this that anyone can copy and use.

You may have discovered from reading parts of my own basketball journey that there are experiences I have had along the way that have had an extreme and lasting impact on me. These experiences have made me think about the game that has been so much of my life and how I can continue to leverage it to increase my contribution to others.

This all leads to the reason why I decided to write this book.

The real motivation came from my last fifteen years of personal contact with parents and kids I have trained, ranging from fourth graders to seniors in high school. Watching how American youth basketball operates at the grassroots level has changed, with its negative impact on so many parents and kids. They so often discover what they didn't know was what would have been best for them during their youth basketball journey. Their regrets have had a lasting impact on me.

In 2003, when I began to manage the basketball programs at Suwanee Sports Academy in the suburbs of Atlanta, I was very naïve about how our youth basketball system had changed. As a college coach I was so engrossed with all that was needed to keep the program successful that the only time I came in contact with youth basketball was when I was recruiting.

As I organized different programs for the Academy, along with bringing in outside groups to rent the facility for tournaments, I witnessed a culture to which I could not relate. It became evident our youth basketball system had totally changed.

Youth basketball no longer emphasized fundamentals as the way to improve. It had shifted to an overemphasis on playing games. This basketball culture has been in effect for three decades, so today's parents know only one way. Many parents and kids are being influenced by the myths for success. So many of these myths are responsible for their child's regrets that come from their youth basketball journey.

Hindsight is always 20-20. As I learned how the youth basketball system had really changed, I discovered why in the mid-90's I recognized a different mentality our players at Georgia Tech had regarding individual improvement in the off-season.

When I started coaching in 1975 at Appalachian State, I learned how complex it was to be a coach. The one thing I knew for sure was what I needed to do to help a player get better and reach for their full potential. It was a simple formula. Once players understood, they accepted the only way they could get better was by focusing on their own skills training.

I was always proud as I watched players who bought into how to get better as they moved through our program along with so many moving onto solid careers in the NBA. Those moments began to almost disappear as we began getting players who were All Americans, but grew up in this new way of thinking and believing individual improvement was accomplished differently. Their idea on how to improve was playing pickup games in the off-season. This led to very little improvement, and missing out on having NBA careers.

As I reflect back on my past college coaching experiences, I know I am telling you about All Americans who became future NBA players, but it is all relevant that no matter what the player's age, it comes down to having the correct mindset to improve as a player.

My enjoyment from coaching has never changed, and will not stop. It is all about teaching and guiding individuals. This is why I continue to inform parents and players on the correct approach for how to get better and reach their potential while participating in basketball.

It deeply concerns me as I watch kids enjoy playing basketball that I know they don't know they are not receiving the guidance needed to fulfill a dream. Basic fundamentals and individual skill development are the building blocks of basketball. Everything on the court depends on the execution of basic skills. Proper execution of team skills depends on fundamentals and individual skill improvement, not how well plays are practiced.

My vision for this book is not to change the youth basketball system. My vision is to inform and teach as many parents as I can connect with that there is a better way. My mission is to help parents and kids get on a path that will enable them to reach their potential and their dreams of playing the great game of basketball.

I believe it is possible. Do I believe this is going to take some time? Absolutely. This book is the first step. It will put you on the right path, with everything you need to play the right role in guiding your child through the youth basketball journey.

It's Your Time to Get Started

N ow it's your turn. I know I have covered a lot of ground throughout this book with you. The blueprint I have given you has been proven. It works. It will work for you and your child. I have lived this approach with parents and players for many years. The formula just has to be followed.

Writing this book and sharing my knowledge with you, I have to tell you, has been an amazing experience for me. I really love the game of basketball because of the huge impact I can make on so many parents and kids through the sport, as well as seeing the positive impact kid's gain because of the life lessons learned through their participation in the game.

Take what I have shared and just get started. It's all about taking small steps, and about taking action. It's great that you've read this book, and now you know so much more about how to help your child become successful. But you have to move into action.

So, where do you go from here? What do you do next?

While you are assimilating everything you have learned in this book, consider these questions. They will guide you towards specific next steps.

Now that you have finished this book, do you feel like you have a good grasp on the blueprint for success? Are you confident you have what you need to take next steps on your own with the information you have?

If your answer is yes, while you are assimilating everything I have shared in the book, I suggest you take the following actions to get started. You can refresh your recollection by re-reading parts of the book.

Parents with Pre-High School Kids Playing Youth Basketball

1. Your approach for individual development - Hire an instructor who can teach the basic skills of footwork, dribbling and shooting correctly and is capable of setting up individual practice plans so your child can work alone.
2. Participate in Travel Ball - Join a team with a limited schedule. Don't allow your child to play too many games and not have the time to work on his own individual skill development.
3. Determine a plan for your responsibilities during and after competition. Decide on the individual statistics you will track during games you attend and how you will handle your post-game comments.

Parents with Kids Playing High School Basketball

I recommend you focus on the same three actions listed for the pre-high school kids above. I also suggest the following two items:

1. Focus on the college level you expect your child to be able to play. Then, begin to track the college programs on that level with needs that fit the type of player like your child.
2. Consider the best strategy for the right time for your child to get on a college coach's radar. Remember some of the considerations in Chapter 23. These strategies include sponsored Travel Team, information packets for college coaches, special relationships which can be leveraged, summer camps to attend and campus visits which should be made.

If you would like a little more help while assimilating everything I have shared with you in the book and how best to get started from here, learn more at www. KevinCantwellBasketball.com.

If you would like to learn more about working directly with me and my team, you can find out more by visiting www.KevinCantwellBasketball.com.

Whatever is best for you, the most important thing is to start. Take action now. You are armed with everything you need to take the next step. It is your time. It is your turn.

For those of you who decide to continue the journey of discovery on your own, I wish you the best of luck. Please reach out and let me know how you are doing with what I have taught you in this book. Don't hesitate to check in with any questions if I can be of further assistance.

If you want to consider how I can join you and provide more support on your journey for ensuring your child has a positive experience playing the game of basketball, learn more by visiting www.KevinCantwellBasketball.com

Parent's Guide to Youth Basketball and Beyond: How to Navigate Your Child's Path to College Basketball is proven. It will work for you. Just follow the steps I gave you throughout this book.

Tell me about your success story. You can reach me at www.KevinCantwell Basketball.com

Be sure to access bonus content as my gift to you

www.KevinCantwellBasketball.com/p/gifts

About the Authors

Kevin Cantwell

Kevin Cantwell has been recruiting and developing basketball players at all levels of the game for nearly 40 years. Kevin has established key relationships with coaches, players, scouts, and others in the sport in the United States and abroad. Today he uses his knowledge, experience and relationship networks to help parents enhance the basketball and life experience for their kids.

Kevin's passion and knowledge for teaching the game helped put the Suwanee Sports Academy in metro Atlanta on the map as a nationally recognized brand for its approach to training and operating successful basketball events.

In addition to his immense knowledge and dedication to grassroots basketball, Kevin spent 28 years as a college basketball coach and recruiter. During his career, he spent 14 years as Associate Head Coach at Georgia Tech under legendary coach Bobby

Cremins. Kevin was considered one of the best recruiters in college basketball during his coaching career. While at Georgia Tech, he recruited and coached 22 NBA players, and helped guide the Yellow Jackets to the Final Four in 1990.

Kevin began his coaching career at Appalachian State University as an Assistant Coach and also served as Head Coach for five seasons. He earned a Bachelor's Degree in Social Science from UNC-Asheville, and a Master's Degree in Physical Education from Appalachian State.

Kevin lives in the Western Carolina Mountains in Lake Junaluska, North Carolina with his wife, Cathy.

Pat Alacqua

Pat Alacqua has been building his own businesses or supporting other entrepreneurs as they navigate the building of their successful enterprises for close to 40 years. He is energized by the challenges of business creation and development from entrepreneur to enterprise.

Pat has a passion for creating positive change within the youth sports landscape. Over the years, he has helped train kids of all ages, including coaching a nationally competitive Travel Team and serving as a coach for a successful high school basketball program in Georgia. He navigated the basketball journey for both his own son and daughter. His son went on to have a solid college basketball career. Pat's basketball player development knowledge and experience continue to guide his focus for exploring new ways to match his love of sports and passion for business building.

Supporting the development of athletes and building successful entrepreneurial businesses motivated Pat and an investment group to acquire Suwanee Sports Academy in 2002. As Managing Partner and CEO, Pat developed the business turnaround plan, and created the long-term strategy and business model used to build The Academy into a nationally recognized brand. He sold his ownership interests in The Sports Academy in 2011 after developing a solid leadership team and sustainable growth strategy.

Pat also was co-founding entrepreneur of a global tradeshow and event management company recognized as the leading service company in its market segment. His innovative approach to servicing customers, operational planning and workforce training are still utilized today by companies in the tradeshow and event industry. He guided the company for more than 20 years until it was sold in 2001. Pat was inducted into the EACA (Exhibitor Appointed Contractor Association) Hall of Fame in 2006.

Pat lives in Johns Creek, Georgia, with his wife, Elaine.

Made in the USA
Middletown, DE
15 March 2018